1001
Questions
to Ask Before
You Get
MARRIED

MONICA MENDEZ LEAHY

McGraw·Hill

New York   Chicago   San Francisco   Lisbon   London   Madrid   Mexico City
Milan   New Delhi   San Juan   Seoul   Singapore   Sydney   Toronto

Library of Congress Cataloging-in-Publication Data

Leahy, Monica Mendez.
    1,001 questions to ask before you get married / Monica Mendez Leahy.
        p.   cm.
    ISBN 0-07-143803-3 (alk. paper)
      1. Mate Selection—Miscellanea.   2. Couples—Miscellanea.   3. Marriage—
Miscellanea.   I. Title: One thousand one questions to ask before you get married.
II. Title: One thousand and one questions to ask before you get married.   III. Title.

HQ801.L345   2004
646.7′7—dc22   2003022473

8 9 0   DOC/DOC   3 2 1 0 9 8

ISBN 0-07-143803-3

McGraw-Hill books are available at special quantity discounts to use as premiums and
sales promotions, or for use in corporate training programs. For more information, please
write to the Director of Special Sales, Professional Publishing, McGraw-Hill, Two Penn
Plaza, New York, NY 10121-2298. Or contact your local bookstore.

This book is printed on acid-free paper.

To my husband, Robert, thank you for proofreading, correcting, and giving me indispensable advice. Your help was priceless, your patience enviable, and the love you show me every day, a true blessing. And to my parents, who gave the world the best gift possible—happy children. Words can never express the love I feel for all of you.

Contents

Part 7 • **Leisure Time**   95

Part 8 • **Finances**   109

Part 9 • **Physical Intimacy**   131

Acknowledgments

Above all, I want to acknowledge the countless individuals who shared with me their personal stories of romantic successes and failures. The advice, admonitions, and anecdotes provided by these men and women of various ages are the basis for this work. I thank them for their contributions and hope that in writing this book they will be among the last to lament, "If only I had known then what I know now" in describing their own marriages.

I must also acknowledge the tireless work of Diane Sollee, the founder and director of the Coalition for Marriage, Family, and Couples Education (CMFCE), also known as Smart Marriages. Her organization and website provided a tremendous amount of information and links to medical research papers, government statistics, and recently published articles. My heartfelt gratitude goes out to her and to all those who have devoted their professional lives to studying and writing about how to develop healthy and happy relationships.

This book would not be in print without the encouragement and assistance of Stephany Evans of the Imprint Agency and Michele Pezzuti of McGraw-Hill. Their enthusiasm and belief in the importance of getting this information into the hands of couples everywhere gave the project the fuel it needed to take off.

Recognition must also be given to my husband, Robert. His collaboration on this project was an essential part of the journey from idea to printed page. His clear thoughts and articulate explanations offered an illuminating male perspective on several subjects. Our lengthy conversations sparked several ideas and challenged many assumptions. I will never take for granted how fortunate I am to be with a man who's such a pleasure to talk with.

Introduction

On my wedding day, my eighty-two-year-old grandmother pulled me aside and, in a voice that was almost a whisper, said, "When I got married, all I did was cry for the first two years!" A few hours later, my new husband's grandmother came up to me and said, "Dear, now that you're family, I would like to share something with you." Thinking it was going to be her family's famous recipe for peach cobbler, I was startled to hear her say, "When I first got married, all I did was cry for about two years!" Since my grandmother doesn't speak English, and my husband's grandmother doesn't know a word of Spanish, I knew they weren't in cahoots.

I had heard that the first few years of marriage were usually a period of adjustment, but in my love-struck mind I assumed "adjusting" meant having the love of my life nearby twenty-four hours a day. Now that was an adjustment I was looking forward to! Needless to say, I was setting myself up for a rude awakening.

The newlywed shock that my husband and I felt was a shared hypersensitivity to our actions and any decisions we were forced to make. Several couples I spoke with agreed with this description. One husband described his wariness in this way: "I was afraid to help with the dishes. Because if I did, I thought I would have to do the dishes every day for the rest of my life."

We did notice that the problems my husband and I worked through easily were the ones that we had anticipated and openly discussed prior to getting married. I realized then that few individuals are prepared for the realities of married life. I strongly believe that there should be an extended guidebook of real-life scenarios to help couples discuss their compatibility and plans for their future. From this idea this book was born.

The questions in the forthcoming pages were drafted based on the real concerns, causes of separation, endearing anecdotes, challenges, and triumphs that I've heard from hundreds of couples from all walks of life. I'm happy to pass along their advice, in the form of 1,001 questions, from one friend to another.

How to Use This Book

Warning: Do not attempt to complete this book in one day!

A book as all-inclusive as this will give even the most devoted couple "inquiry overload" if they try answering even half the questions in one day.

Go at your own pace. The given sequence is recommended, but not required. You may find that you and your partner are comfortable only going through one chapter or one section at a time. You may even prefer answering some questions by yourself, and then casually bring them up in conversations with your partner.

Whenever you do decide to approach a subject, make sure you're alone, relaxed, and are open in mind and spirit for a personal conversation. Distractions such as watching TV or chatting with a group of friends compromise your answers. They take away from the attention, reflection, and privacy needed to give honest and insightful responses.

Following are some suggestions that will help you maximize the benefits this book offers.

Answer Each Question Honestly

This book is not a test to see how many questions you and your partner can answer alike. There are no right or wrong answers either. The purposes of these questions are simply to disclose how you would act under a given situation and to give insight to your views of the past and future. Don't temper your answers to please your partner. Don't give a response that sounds very diplomatic, but doesn't reflect the truth. Giving dishonest answers in order to keep the peace does no one any favors.

Only Answer for Yourself

This book is about discovery. It's set up to find out who you and your partner are and what you expect out of marriage. Resist the temptation to answer for your partner. If a question asks for your opinion, don't answer with a response that describes your partner. For example, if the question asks "Do you want children?" don't respond with "Jerry doesn't want children." Concentrate on discovering who you really are, and what you really want. It's only when you know this about yourself that you can decide if your partner can help you accomplish what you want for your future. Which leads us to our next tip.

Clarify What You Want and What You Expect

Your answers should clarify what you expect from each other in your marriage. They can also allow you to express your priorities and what behaviors you're not willing to give up. If you're an unapologetic slob around the house and don't intend to change, let your partner know up front.

Don't Aim for Change

Listen to each other's responses without interfering. The exercises were created for you to learn about each other, not try to change each other. When you've completed this book, you will have a priceless cache of responses that will help you answer the most important question: "Can I live with what my partner has to offer without counting on him (or her) to change?"

Don't Be Discouraged

If after completing a few chapters you've found that you and your partner haven't answered very many questions alike, don't despair. Lack of differences is not the key to marital success. It's how you deal with these differences that will determine the longevity of your marriage. When you and your partner disagree on the answer to a question, use the guidelines laid out in "How to Discuss Your Differences." They will help you manage discrepancies that you may find along the way.

How to Discuss Your Differences

Putting all your cards on the table in front of your partner is cathartic. You're telling your partner, "This is who I am. Here's the good and bad." A weight is lifted from your shoulders when you've presented yourself honestly. You put the ball in your partner's court allowing him or her to make a decision to accept you without any misconception. The questions throughout this book will allow you and your partner to reach this level of full disclosure.

So what do you do when you don't like what you hear? What if you don't agree with your partner's answers? Discovering differences doesn't mean throwing in the towel on your relationship. A lack of opposing views has never been the secret to a successful marriage. A disagreement with your partner is an opportunity to hone diversity management skills.

Notice I did not say conflict resolution skills. Discussing differences doesn't have to be a conflict. Becoming frustrated, angry, and confused with your partner is natural. You probably get that way with friends, your boss, and even your dog. But, unless you're overly aggressive, these diverse points of view are managed without conflict.

The steps below offer an excellent technique on how to work through differences you may encounter as a couple. Their additional value is that they're applicable to any relationship, both personal and professional.

Discussing Your Differences

Step 1: Think. It's surprising that this is rarely mentioned as the first step in resolving disputes when it is, by far, the most important. Before a single word is uttered, stop and think: "Does this really bother me?" "Can I live with this behavior year after year?" "What am I really angry about?" "Am I angry that she goes out with friends, or do I just hate being alone on a Friday night?" Think, and try to pinpoint the cause of friction. You should be able to explain your dilemma in just one sentence. Are you angry because you think he's lazy, or do you just want him to take out the trash? There's a big difference.

Step 2: Decide. Once you've established the exact reason for your anger, decide if, when, and how you will present your case. First, decide if change is possible, reasonable, or influenced by outside factors. Was it really your partner who made you cranky, or just work-related stress? Are you being unreasonable for asking your bartending spouse to not work evenings?

Second, decide when you want to bring up the discussion. There's no rule that states differences must be discussed the instant they appear. Choose a time when you can give each other your full attention. Bringing up sensitive topics when you're both tired and cranky is not a good idea. Also, think back to when you last had a disagreement. If you're constantly annoyed and asking for changes, go back to Step 1 and think of the reasons for your unhappiness.

Third, go over in your mind how you will explain your feelings and request change. Strive to present your case in the clearest and least-offensive way possible. A soft approach works best, and will be further discussed in Chapter 64, "The Friendship Factor."

Step 3: KISS. That's right, KISS—as in Keep It Short and Simple. Start with a positive (e.g., "Honey, I know how careful you are with money."), then state your feelings (e.g., "However, I really feel we should balance our checkbook so we don't bounce checks.") That's it.

- Do not go on and on. Rambling doesn't make you more convincing. It just makes your partner tune out.
- Do not use poisonous phrases. Saying "You never . . . ," "You always . . . ," or "If you loved me you would . . ." kills credibility. Not only are these statements probably untrue, but using them comes off as manipulative.
- Do not get off the subject. If you're arguing about who will balance the checkbook, only talk about the checkbook. Leave out opinions concerning the bank or how much money you partner spends. Don't get distracted. If it doesn't directly involve the checkbook, don't bring it up.
- Do not get personal or take cheap shots. The only thing that hitting below the belt will accomplish is that you'll both become angrier.

I can't emphasize this more: When speaking, direct your words toward the behavior, not the person. Be polite and gentle in your approach. Avoid starting a sentence with "You" or "You're," since it comes off as accusatory. For example, instead of saying, "You spend too much time with your family," try "I would like for us to spend more time together and less time with your family."

Step 4: Listen. Give your partner a chance to respond without interruption. Listen to what that person is saying. Try to understand his opinion, but don't focus on having your point understood. Show that you have been listening by paraphrasing statements when it's your turn to respond. For example say, "You said you don't like it when I use your razor, so I will buy my own blades."

Step 5: Agree on an ending. Guide conversations toward an end result. Keep an open mind. Be flexible and compromising. You'll have better success at resolving disagreements if you agree to small changes, and take them one step at a time. Don't demand more than either one of you is capable of giving. You can't turn a slob into a neat freak. However, you can work out a solution that gets her to put her dirty clothes in the hamper. Learn to know when to "let it go." Do not harbor resentment the rest of the day or week over a disagreement.

Dos and Don'ts When Discussing Answers

- Do not try to discuss all of your answers in one day.
- Don't get defensive: "What do you mean I have a spending problem?"
- Do acknowledge your partner's feelings even if you don't agree: "I'm interested why you believe my spending is out of control. When you're through, I'll give you reasons why I disagree."
- Don't do the turn-around game: "I'm not rude. You're the one that insults my family."
- Do address comments directly and without accusations: "Why do you feel my actions were offensive?"
- Don't use guilt to get your way: "After all I've done for you, why won't you do this little favor for me?"
- Do avoid provoking guilt. It builds resentment and eventually backfires.
- Don't criticize the person: "You're so stubborn."
- Do criticize the action: "Stubbornness makes it difficult to compromise."
- Don't dismiss your partner's feelings: "Quit whining. Nothing's wrong!"
- Do listen to your partner's concerns and offer to help: "What can we do to ease your worries?"
- Don't give your partner the silent treatment.

- Don't have a "my way or the highway" attitude.
- Do approach each discussion as a team effort to find a solution.
- Don't make cruel or vindictive statements to get back at your partner.
- Do pause or take a time-out if you feel the conversation has become too emotionally charged.

Time after time, these steps have been shown to keep disputes from escalating into bitter feuds. Practicing these steps will help you and your partner work through any disagreement.

Part 1

Your Past

"I tend to live in the past because
most of my life is there."

—Herb Caen

Realizing where you came from, how it shaped you, and what you want in life are the first steps in preparing for marriage. We tend to follow the example of our parents. If you're happy with the example they gave you, then you have a blueprint on what to look for in a partner. If you didn't like the relationships that you saw growing up, you can take steps to prevent falling into the same patterns.

Look closely at the relationship skills of the people you and your partner grew up with. Remember the attributes that created strong and happy bonds, and those that caused pain. Determine the conditions and attitudes that led these individuals into unhappy relationships. Learn from others' mistakes as well as their successes while not falling into the trap of comparing yourselves or measuring yourselves against them. Decide how you and your spouse will incorporate the positive while avoiding the negative.

Take life's lessons and use them to create a strong and loving marriage.

Growing Up in a Traditional Family

Although recent headlines report the death of the two-parent household, America is still largely made up of the traditional nuclear family. If you were blessed with two happily married parents, then you've been fortunate to have a front-row seat in observing what it takes to make a marriage successful.

With your partner, read each question, allowing each person to express his or her answer without interruption. Discuss if and how the answers given will affect your marriage.

1. What do you believe was the bond that kept your parents married?
2. What characteristics of your parents' marriage would you like to see in yours?
3. What characteristics of your parents' marriage would you like to avoid?
4. How did your mother treat your father and vice versa?
5. Do you and your partner want to treat each other the same way your parents treated each other?
6. In your family, who was the main decision maker?

7. Would you like your marriage to follow this pattern as well?
8. Would you describe your parents as living in traditional male/female roles?
9. Do you aspire to hold traditional male/female roles in your household?
10. Would you describe your parents' relationship as one-sided or a true partnership?
11. Would you best describe your parents' relationship as being positive, passive, or poisonous?
12. Did you see your parents work through difficult periods in their marriage?
13. Did your parents avoid any type of disagreements or confrontations?
14. Has your parents' marriage affected how you address problems with your partner?
15. Did your parents argue often?
16. If your parents argued, was it a sign of a troubled marriage, or was it just their way of communicating?
17. Did your parents spent most of their leisure time together, or apart?
18. Did one parent constantly tease, belittle, or humiliate the other?
19. Did your parents frequently laugh together?
20. Were you aware of one parent hiding items or keeping secrets from the other?

Growing Up with Divorced or Single Parents

If most of your formative years were spent with a single parent or divorced parents, research shows an increase in the likelihood that you will divorce or become a single parent as well. This doesn't mean that your fate is sealed. Educating yourself on the reasons why your parents' relationship did not succeed—and avoiding the same behaviors—increases your chance that history will not repeat itself in your marriage.

With your partner, read each question out loud. Allow each person to voice his or her answer without interruptions. Discuss if and how the answers given will affect your marriage.

1. If you were raised by a single parent, did you know a couple that served as a role model for a successful long-term relationship?
2. If raised by a single parent, did you miss having a father or mother growing up?

3. Were several members of your family single parents while you were growing up?
4. Did your single parent stress independence and self-reliance?
5. Did your single parent frequently comment that you can't trust or rely on others?
6. Have you developed a relationship with both of your biological parents?
7. If your parents are divorced, what do you believe was the cause of their divorce?
8. Do you blame either parent or yourself for the breakup of their marriage?
9. If your parents are divorced, do you fear the same outcome for your relationship?
10. If your parents are divorced, what have you learned that will help you avoid the same fate?
11. How did the divorce affect your views about marriage or lifelong intimate relationships?
12. Do you feel the divorce had a positive or a negative effect on you and your family?
13. What do you believe is the primary cause of divorce in general?
14. Are most of your family members (aunts, uncles, siblings) divorced?
15. Have your parents maintained a good, or at least civil, relationship with each other?
16. Did your mother or father use you or your siblings as tools to obtain information about the other parent?
17. Do you want your partner to become the mother or father figure you desired while growing up?
18. Did your parents actively date others or have more than one or two relationships after they were divorced? If so, how do you think this affects your view of marriage?

19. Did you witness your parents encourage other couples to separate or get a divorce?
20. Did you take advantage of your parents' separation by using guilt or their infrequent communication to get things you wanted?

Impact and Influences
of Other Relationships

Parents aren't only the two people whose genes you possess. There are adoptive parents, stepparents, and other guardians. If your mother or father did not raise you, the word *parent* will refer to the person or people who had the strongest influence in your upbringing.

With your partner, read each question out loud. Allow each person to voice his or her answer without interruptions. Discuss if and how the answers given will affect your marriage.

1. Growing up, were you exposed to mostly positive and loving relationships?
2. Did conversations among friends and family mainly involve complaining about the shortcomings of others?
3. Did you witness any physical, emotional, or sexual abuse in your household while growing up?
4. Did those close to you believe that marriage was a burden or a joy?
5. Was getting married seen as a mandatory goal that you must achieve in life?

6. Were you aware of any infidelity by either of your parents or other family members?
7. If "yes" to the above, how did the spouse who was cheated on react and deal with this situation?
8. What effect did the infidelity have on you and other family members?
9. Growing up, did your family believe in a double standard between the sexes?
10. Were you often told that the opposite sex was not to be trusted or respected?
11. Do you want your marriage to resemble a relationship portrayed on TV or in the movies? If so describe this relationship.
12. Name a couple that you know who have a great marriage. What attributes of their marriage would you like to emulate?
13. Did your friends and family spoil you? Did you usually get what you wanted?
14. Did you feel you didn't get enough attention from others? Are you looking for that attention from your partner?
15. Were you regularly exposed to situations in which men and women could socialize with each other?
16. Did you ever suffer the loss of a family member? If so, how did you cope with your grief?

At School and Play

It's undeniable that interacting with childhood friends and classmates influences how you relate to others as an adult. How you treated people in your past, even as a child, is probably similar to how you treat people today.

With your partner, take turns answering each question below.

1. Were you jealous of some of your friends while growing up? If so, how and why?
2. Were you ever told that you were a player? If so, how did that make you feel?
3. Were you determined to be popular in school? Were you popular?
4. Did you enjoy going to school, or did you feel it was a waste of time?
5. Did you like your teachers? If so, which ones and why?
6. Did you cause disruptions in the classroom? If so, describe them.
7. Did you frequently get into fights with your classmates?
8. Which subjects were your favorites in school and why?
9. Were you a good, average, or poor student? What made you excel or lose interest in your studies?

10. Were you involved in sports as a child? If so, how did you get along with your teammates and coaches?
11. Did you ever seek revenge against someone while growing up?
12. Were you a late bloomer or forced to mature faster than others while growing up?
13. Describe an unpleasant childhood memory that still bothers you.
14. Describe a pleasant childhood memory that made an impact on your life.
15. What is the worst trouble you ever got into as a child?
16. Describe the types of children you spent time with while growing up. How would they describe you as a child?
17. Would you like to relive your childhood? Why or why not?
18. Describe your first childhood crush.
19. Were you picked on as a child? Did you pick on others?
20. Did you ever run away from home?

Your Past

Thoughts on Your Answers

When looking for a life partner, we look for someone not only to share our future, but also to address part of our past. If we admired a parent or other relative who was well off, we most likely sought a partner who was financially stable. Likewise, we also look for someone to fill a void we felt growing up. If you felt your upbringing was too serious, and you craved laughter and humor, you may seek a partner who amuses you and can make you laugh.

Your answers to these exercises about the past are important because they help you and your partner identify scenarios that brought joy and those that brought pain. By discussing these events, you can decide what you need to do to create a happy home life. When going over each of your answers, keep in mind the following:

- **The overall tone of answers given.** A majority of happy and positive answers can mean you're at peace with your past. You probably want a marriage like the ones you have seen growing up. An overall negative tone in your responses could mean a lingering anger or resentment over your past. Discuss how this anger can be resolved, and how you believe it can affect your expectations of married life.

- **The type of relationship each of you would like to emulate.** When asked whose marriage you would like yours to resemble, did you or your partner describe a real or fictitious couple? Was it a couple that you spent a lot of time with, or one that you only saw portrayed on television? Good relationship role models don't necessarily have to come from one couple. You can hope to copy several different traits held by a variety of couples. You may aspire to have the passion seen in one couple, and the thriftiness seen in another.

- **What you and your partner perceive as a "normal" household.** Normalcy is in the eye of the beholder. If you grew up seeing couples frequently yelling at each other, but otherwise having loving long-term relationships, you may think yelling at your partner is a normal way of expressing your thoughts. Your partner, on the other hand, may come from a quieter upbringing, and believes yelling is only appropriate when the house is burning down. The answers you have given in the previous chapters described the household you and your partner grew up in. If they are very different from each other, or if you are uncomfortable with how your partner was raised, then you both need to discuss what behaviors you will and will not be repeating in your marriage.

Part 2

Parents and In-Laws

"No matter how calmly you try to referee, parenting will eventually produce bizarre behavior, and I'm not talking about the kids."

—Bill Cosby, *Fatherhood*, 1986

Making your marriage priority number one is not without sacrifice. With only twenty-four hours in a day, couples soon find that it's impossible to be all things to all people. While it is important to devote time to others, make sure to devote time to each other.

Sometimes the people most demanding of your time will be parents and in-laws. Beware of establishing patterns such as having dinner with one set of parents every Friday, or always volunteering to help with home repair projects. Your life as a married couple will change in ways you did not anticipate. The routine you and your spouse carried on before you were married will be altered. Although you and your spouse may understand and agree to these changes, parents may voice strong objections that put a strain on your marriage.

The job of integrating the families rests on the newlyweds. Diplomacy, resiliency, and unity as a couple are a must. Important decisions should be made with your spouse, not your parents. Present yourselves as an inseparable team. Let parents and in-laws know that you remain their son or daughter, but are now their *married* son or daughter, with new priorities and responsibilities.

Always treat your in-laws with the same love and respect you show your spouse.

Your Parents

Few enter a marriage free of parents. Whether you love them, avoid them, or never got to know them, they will be a part of your married life. To what extent parents will be involved in your marriage is often a subject of debate and disagreement.

Working separately, write down your answers to the questions below. The questions refer to each person's own parents, not the in-laws. When finished, discuss your answers and how you believe they may positively or negatively affect your marriage.

1. Do your parents approve or disapprove of your partner?
2. Is it important that your parents like your partner?
3. If your parents don't approve of your partner, how will it affect your marriage?
4. Will you or your partner look for ways to resolve this disapproval?
5. If your parents and your partner have a disagreement, whose side will you most likely take?
6. Whom would you rather disappoint, your parents or your partner?
7. What would you do if your parents intentionally or unintentionally criticize or offend your partner?

8. What would you do if your partner said he or she did not like your parents, and would rather not spend time with them?
9. Do your parents have a strong opinion on how you should live your married life?
10. Do you plan on living with your parents at any time during your marriage?
11. Will you financially support your parents when they retire or if they become unable to support themselves?
12. How do you feel about asking your parents for financial support?
13. With which family members, if any, do you plan on spending the various holidays?
14. Is it more important to have a good relationship with your parents or your partner?
15. Does your partner feel that you're too attached to your parents?
16. Would you be willing to move to a location far away from your family?
17. In general, whose advice would you most likely take, your partner's or your parents'?
18. If your parents criticize your choice of married lifestyle, how will you respond?
19. Would you agree to have an aged or ill parent move in with you?
20. Will you be spending more time with or money on your parents than your in-laws?
21. If you and your partner have a disagreement, will you seek solace in your parents?

Your In-Laws

t is understandable if you and your partner each feel more comfortable with your own parents than with your in-laws. After all, you've probably known them all your life. Your in-laws may be strangers you've just met. Yet, always remember your in-laws are your partner's parents. Putting down or insulting them is no different than if someone insulted your own parents.

Working separately, you and your partner are to write down answers to the questions below. When finished, discuss your answers and how you both believe they may positively or negatively affect your relationship with each other as a married couple.

1. Do you feel your in-laws approve of you as a partner? Whether they do or not, how does that make you feel?
2. If your in-laws disagree with you, how would you feel if your partner did not take your side?
3. If you were having problems with your in-laws, would you speak to them directly without consulting your partner?
4. Should your partner be in charge of resolving problems you may have with your in-laws?

5. If your in-laws offend you (intentionally or unintentionally), would you speak up immediately or expect your partner to defend you on the spot?
6. How do you feel about financially supporting your in-laws when they retire or become unable to support themselves?
7. How do you feel about spending holidays with your in-laws instead of your parents?
8. How important is it to please your in-laws?
9. If you had to decide on spending the day with your parents or in-laws, which would you choose?
10. Would you prefer to live in a different city or state than your in-laws?
11. Do you feel uncomfortable if your partner spends time alone with his or her parents?
12. Do you feel your in-laws are a bad influence on your relationship with your partner?
13. Do you feel pressure to dress, talk, or behave differently around your in-laws?
14. Do you expect to get a phone call or a gift from your in-laws on your birthday?
15. Would you be offended if gifts received from your in-laws were not as expensive or generous as the ones they gave to your partner?
16. Do you feel your parents treat your partner better than your in-laws treat you? If so, how?
17. If you were having a dispute with your in-laws, would you forbid your partner from having contact with them?
18. Do you expect an inheritance from your in-laws?
19. Do you feel your in-laws have too strong an influence on your partner's thoughts and actions?
20. What positive contributions, if any, have your in-laws made to your relationship with your partner? What about negative contributions?

Are We Our Parents?

Is there truth to the statement "The apple doesn't fall far from the tree"? Do men marry women who remind them of their mothers? Do women marry men who remind them of their fathers? Whatever you believe, every adult experiences a moment where he recognizes a parent in himself.

Working individually, answer the questions below.

	Physically Height, body type, hair and eye color, etc.	Emotionally What you worry about, what makes you laugh or cry, etc.	In Your Actions How you act when you are angry or stressed, etc.	Other Ways Hobbies, quirks, favorite foods or sayings, etc.
How do you resemble . . .				
your mother?				
your father?				
your mother-in-law?				
your father-in-law?				
How does your partner resemble . . .				
his or her mother?				
his or her father?				
your mother?				
your father?				

8

Spending Time
with Parents

The questionnaire below asks how often you would like to attend certain common events. Make a copy for yourself and your partner. Working separately, enter the letter that best explains how often you would like to participate in the suggested activity, and if you expect to be together or alone. Use the following codes: *A* for at every opportunity; *O* for only if convenient; *R* for rarely; *N* for never; *D* for daily; *W* for weekly; *M* for monthly; *Y* for yearly. When finished, compare answers.

How often would you like to . . .	I'll Do This Alone	We'll Do This Together
visit your parents?		
visit your in-laws?		
go on vacation with your parents?		
go on vacation with your in-laws?		
borrow money from your parents?		
borrow money from your in-laws?		
take your parents out to eat?		
take your in-laws out to eat?		

How often would you like to . . .	I'll Do This Alone	We'll Do This Together
give money to your parents?		
give money to your in-laws?		
ask for marital advice from your parents?		
ask for marital advice from your in-laws?		
give gifts (birthday, anniversary, etc.) to your parents?		
give gifts (birthday, anniversary, etc.) to your in-laws?		
assist your parents with home maintenance or repair projects?		
assist your in-laws with home maintenance or repair projects?		
run simple errands for your parents?		
run simple errands for your in-laws?		
call or e-mail your parents?		
call or e-mail your in-laws?		
borrow items from your parents?		
borrow items from your in-laws?		
enter into business with your parents?		
enter into business with your in-laws?		

9

One Big Happy Family

No matter how close someone is with his or her parents, situations arise that can cause disagreements or friction in your marriage. When this happens, decisions about how much inconvenience you are willing to accept or where your loyalty lies will need to be made.

With your partner, discuss how each of you would handle the situations below. Keep in mind that there are no right or wrong answers.

1. Your mother-in-law has invited you over for dinner. Unfortunately, you don't like her cooking. You
   a. thank her, and then tell her the truth.
   b. say you're on a doctor-supervised diet and can't eat her cooking.
   c. offer to take her out to dinner or cook for her instead.
   d. force yourself to eat her food out of politeness.
2. Your in-laws keep framed photos of your spouse with an old love on the wall. You
   a. couldn't care less. The past is the past.
   b. have your spouse insist they put the pictures away.

    c. refuse to enter their home until the pictures are removed.

    d. tell your in-laws that the pictures hurt your feelings, and you would like them removed.

3. Your in-laws insist you name your first child after a certain relative. You have other plans, and your spouse refuses to take sides. You

    a. go along with your in-laws' desires in order to keep peace in the family.

    b. kindly but firmly let them know you have already chosen a different name.

    c. tell your spouse that he or she needs to tell them to mind their own business.

    d. offer to use their requested name as the child's middle name.

4. Since your father's minor operation, he's been calling you several times a day to come over or to run errands. Your spouse has started to complain. You

    a. ask your partner to be more sympathetic about your father's condition.

    b. tell your father you can only help him two or three times each week.

    c. have your father move in with you.

    d. hire an assistant for your father.

5. Your spouse's family get-togethers bore you to tears, and you've been invited to one this weekend. You

    a. refuse to go.

    b. tell your spouse your limit is two or three get-togethers a year.

    c. say you have to work.

    d. go, and take a good book or spend the time in front of the television.

6. Your parents have given substantial financial assistance to a sibling who always seems to have money problems. You
   a. are grateful for not having money problems of your own.
   b. demand that your parents give all their children equal support or none at all.
   c. say nothing but be resentful.
   d. cut all contact with your parents.

7. Your in-laws gave you an outfit that you feel silly wearing. They have requested you wear it to an upcoming family function. You
   a. lie and say it's being altered or at the dry cleaners.
   b. say you appreciate the gift, but it's not your style.
   c. wear it for them, then give it away.
   d. thank them, but tell them you'll be exchanging it for something you like better.

8. After house sitting, your parents kept a copy of your house keys. You
   a. ask for the keys back.
   b. do nothing.
   c. change the locks.
   d. hook up video surveillance cameras and buy a guard dog.

9. Although you've requested they stop dropping by unannounced, your parents and in-laws continue to do so. You
   a. hang a "Do not disturb" sign on the door.
   b. pretend you're not home and refuse to open the door.
   c. invite them in, since they *are* family.
   d. answer the door naked to teach them a lesson.

10. Your visiting parents (or in-laws) would like to stay with you and your spouse for three weeks. You
    a. agree. After all, they've been very generous to you and your spouse.
    b. offer to let them stay, but for only one week.
    c. suggest they stay at a nearby hotel.
    d. tell them the plumbing is being repaired, so you can't comfortably have overnight guests.

Parents and In-Laws
Thoughts on Your Answers

Many newlyweds enter marriage with a few misconceptions about their relationships with their parents and in-laws. The first is that their relationship with their own parents will not change. The second is that their parents and in-laws will not have a significant involvement in their marriage. Parents and in-laws will be a part of both your and your partner's lives for as long as they live.

Parents often have the best intentions. Yet, like their children, they have the ability to enhance or to cause aggravation. They may often be available to nurture you. As they age, you may have the opportunity to return the favor and nurture them in return.

When discussing your answers, look for the characteristics mentioned below. Consider whether they describe your relationship now, or if these patterns might develop in the future. If they do exist or you feel they could emerge, decide on whether you will choose to accept them, or what actions you'll take to prevent them from occurring.

Discuss whether your answers in these chapters suggested the following:

- **A stronger devotion to your parents than to your spouse.** It's wonderful to have a close bond with your parents. However, frequent clashes between loyalties could show a person's difficulty in seeing him- or herself as a husband or wife as opposed to his or her parents' adult child. This is common in individuals who prefer living with their parents than alone with their partner. They consult their parents first before making any decisions, and choose their company, instead of their partner's, when accomplishing day-to-day tasks.

- **A persistent and justifiable feeling of being looked down upon by your partner's family.** This is more than just a feeling that your in-laws do not approve of you as a spouse. If you have witnessed a regular pattern of being put down in front of your partner or others, or if you have heard that your future in-laws have tried to dissuade your partner from marrying you, then beware. There's a high likelihood that this behavior will not change. Don't rely on the hope that your partner's family will warm up to you over time. There's little chance that they will, and a big chance that they won't.

- **An obvious bias or strong double standard.** If you or your partner has no problem helping your own relatives, but won't allow the other person to help his, then a double standard exists. Unfortunately, there's more to this inequality than preferential treatment to one's own family or friends. This selfishness often extends to personal items such as property, money, and time. It reflects an attitude summed up by the statement "If it matters to me, it's important. If it matters to you, it's not."

- **The ability to cause chaos or create victims.** Some parents, aside from all the love and positive contributions they've made in their children's lives, have a unique ability to create chaos and stress. Whatever the reasons, simple meetings or brief conversations turn into disagreements, misunderstandings, or full-fledged feuds.

  Inexplicably, these types of people seem to thrive on the disruption they cause. The choice of tactic used, whether guilt, fear, enticement, or disappointment, is not a means to an end, but a way of life.

A wise person once said, "Nobody can take advantage of you without your permission." Take this advice and don't allow others to dictate how you and your spouse are to live your lives. Your best chance at marital happiness is maintaining a balance between strengthening family ties while placing your marriage as priority number one.

Part 3

Significant Others

"All is well with him who is beloved by his neighbors."

—George Herbert

Each person enters a marriage with a preexisting network of friends, family, and professional relationships that can contribute to the strength of a marriage. You must work together to find the right mix of old and new friends. There may be friends and family you enjoy socializing with as a couple, but others you prefer seeing by yourself. Your relationship benefits when you are exposed to people who have successfully created happy and fulfilling lives for themselves and their families.

For you as a newly married couple, the challenge will be to strike a balance between your needs and those of others competing for your time. Compromise is essential when developing or maintaining relationships with friends and family. A picnic with your spouse's best friend who you think is annoying is a fair trade for dinner with your best friend who your spouse thinks is obnoxious.

If this is not the first marriage for either you or your spouse, a unique set of compromises will be integrated into your marriage right from the start. Alimony, child support, and lawyers are ingredients in the stew of obligations that require your time and money. Be careful to ensure that a prior relationship doesn't overshadow your new marriage.

Relatives

Everyone has a different definition of what constitutes a family. For some, family includes only parents and siblings. Others have a much broader definition and include aunts, uncles, cousins, and close friends. How much are you willing to give to accommodate those in your family circle?

Read each question and check the circle that best describes your answer. Allow each person to offer explanations, conditions, or limitations as necessary. Discuss whether you agree with and approve of the answers given.

	Regarding My Relatives		Regarding My Partner's Relatives	
	Yes	No	Yes	No
It's important for me to get to know all relatives well.	○	○	○	○
Relatives are only immediate family members whom I have met.	○	○	○	○
Relatives can only stay over at our house for a few days.	○	○	○	○
Relatives can stay for extended periods (over one month or more) when visiting from out of town.	○	○	○	○
I plan on picking up and dropping off relatives at the airport.	○	○	○	○

	Regarding My Relatives		Regarding My Partner's Relatives	
	Yes	*No*	*Yes*	*No*
I will not pick up relatives at the airport, but will pay for their transportation.	○	○	○	○
I will pay for or cook all the meals while relatives are visiting.	○	○	○	○
I will baby-sit a relative's children free of charge.	○	○	○	○
My partner and I will host large family gatherings.	○	○	○	○
I will employ, or recommend to employers, relatives regardless of whether I know their working style.	○	○	○	○
I will attend all relatives' weddings, birthdays, or other celebrations.	○	○	○	○
I will send gifts (birthday, holiday, graduation, wedding, baby shower, etc.) to relatives.	○	○	○	○
I will lend money to any relative who is having financial difficulties.	○	○	○	○
A relative is welcome to live with us until he or she can get back on his or her feet.	○	○	○	○
Spending time with relatives takes a priority over other previously made arrangements.	○	○	○	○
Sometimes I will speak in a foreign language to my relatives in front of my spouse.	○	○	○	○
I would try to adopt the children of any relative who could no longer care for them.	○	○	○	○
I will become the primary caregiver of a sick aunt, uncle, or cousin.	○	○	○	○

Friends

Y ou may find your group of friends divided three ways: yours, your partner's, and friends you share. Unlike relatives, you choose to build a relationship with these people based on your mutual enjoyment of each other's company.

Work on separate copies of the questionnaire below. When finished, compare answers with your partner. Check off all questions where your partner agrees with the answer you have given.

Would you agree with the following statements?

	Yes	Sometimes	No
I approve of my partner's friends.	○	○	○
I encourage my partner to spend time alone with his or her friends.	○	○	○
My partner's friends are mostly single.	○	○	○
I only permit my partner to see his or her friends when I am present.	○	○	○
My partner discourages me from spending time with my friends.	○	○	○
When my friends and I go out to eat, or for drinks, I usually pick up the check.	○	○	○
My friends believe that my partner and I make a good team.	○	○	○
My friends have warned me about my partner's personality.	○	○	○

	Yes	Sometimes	No
My partner becomes jealous when I socialize with friends of the opposite sex.	○	○	○
One or more friends have tried to get my partner and I to break up.	○	○	○
I totally trust my partner to be alone with members of the opposite sex.	○	○	○
I point out my partner's mistakes in front of others.	○	○	○
My partner is the only friend I have.	○	○	○
If my partner and a friend separately offered to take me out to lunch on the same day, I would go with my friend.	○	○	○
My partner has not introduced me to his or her friends.	○	○	○
I tell my marital problems to my friends.	○	○	○
I don't mind if my partner tells friends our marital problems.	○	○	○
I've known my friends longer than my partner, so I prefer their advice.	○	○	○
I feel more comfortable sharing secrets with my friends than with my partner.	○	○	○
I need to assert my independence by going out alone with friends.	○	○	○
I'm attracted to one or more of my partner's friends.	○	○	○
I feel I can let loose and be myself more with my friends than with my partner.	○	○	○
My partner embarrasses me in front of my friends.	○	○	○
My partner does not try to socialize or fit in with my group of friends.	○	○	○
I'm the only friend my partner has.			
I'd rather hang out with my partner's friends than with my partner.	○	○	○
If my partner and I have a fight, I immediately go to a friend for comfort.	○	○	○

Pets

Anyone who has ever had a pet knows how close the human-to-animal bond can be. Monuments have been built and poems written to commemorate the love for a feathered or furry friend. Be warned, however, that some pets can be possessive. They may resist sharing you with your partner. Or even worse, your partner may resist sharing you with your pet.

With your partner, answer the questions below.

1. Did you have pets growing up?
2. Have you ever had a bad experience with an animal?
3. Will you get any pets after you've married? If so, what kind and how many?
4. Are there any types of pets that you refuse to have?
5. Do you pick up stray animals and care for them?
6. If each of you has pets will they all live with you after you've married?
7. Will you have your pets spayed or neutered?
8. If you had to, could you give up your pets?
9. If your partner has allergies to your pet, what will you do?

10. Do you secretly hate your partner's pets and leave doors or windows open so they can run away?
11. Who will be responsible for the cost and care of your pets?
12. If your pet were hostile towards your partner, what would you do?
13. Do you mistreat your partner's pet in any way while he or she isn't looking?
14. Do you spoil your pets? If so, how?
15. Do you take your dog everywhere? Does this include taking your dog to work or shopping?
16. Will you care for any of your friend's pets or assume ownership if they can't care for them?
17. If your pet caused injury or destruction, would you expect your partner to help pay for the damages? Would you pay if your partner's pet incurred the charges?
18. If your neighbors filed a complaint about your pets, what would you do?
19. Would you let your pets roam around the neighborhood unsupervised?
20. If you wanted to get a pet but your partner didn't approve, what would you do?
21. Has your partner ever threatened to leave if you didn't get rid of your pet? Have you ever threatened to leave your partner over the same issue?

Exes and Past Relationships

Ex-partners are like tattoos—even when you don't see them, you know they're still there. And, like a tattoo that you regret getting, you learn to live with the reminder of your faulty decision. The failure of a first marriage or long-term relationship does not prevent you from having a loving, lasting marriage. Yet, it would be a mistake to believe that your marriage will be free of any reminders of a previous relationship.

With your partner, read each question out loud, answering either True or False.

1. I don't feel that I've had closure with my former partner.
2. I will not allow any contact between my partner and his or her former partner.
3. Because we have a child together, my ex will always be involved in my life.
4. My ex still contacts me on a regular basis.
5. I will continue to share assets with my ex even after I'm remarried.
6. I do not feel threatened by my spouse's former partner.

7. My partner believes that a positive relationship with my ex is important for my children.
8. I find myself frequently talking or thinking about my ex.
9. I've admitted to myself that I am still in love with my ex.
10. I will be inviting my ex to all of my family's functions.
11. Getting married will help me get over my last relationship.
12. My ex-partner has violent tendencies, and I sometimes fear for our safety.
13. In many ways my partner is similar to my ex.
14. I have assumed many debts and other obligations left by my former partner.
15. I'm still very close to my former partner's family and would like to stay in contact with them.
16. Pictures showing my partner or myself with past lovers will be visible in our home.
17. I refuse to live in the same city as my former partner.
18. My partner can attend get-togethers with his former partner's family by himself.
19. I will not allow any money I earn to go toward alimony or child support.
20. I will do everything in my power to make my former partner's life miserable.
21. I foresee lengthy legal battles with my former partner.

Relating to Others

You and your partner may treat each other beautifully, but how do you treat others? Do you admire the way your partner acts in public, or do you find yourself making excuses for his or her behavior?

Take turns answering each of the questions below.

At Work

1. How well do you get along with coworkers? How would they describe you?
2. How well have you gotten along with past and present bosses? How would they describe you?
3. Describe a dispute you had on the job and how it was resolved.
4. Have you ever been reprimanded on the job? If so, what happened? How did you react or resolve the issue?
5. Have you ever been fired or laid off? If so, what were the circumstances?
6. If you're a manager, what's your managerial style?
7. How do you treat customers or clients?

8. Do you volunteer to help others, even if it's not part of your job description?
9. How heavily do you participate in office gossip?
10. Have you ever tried to sabotage a coworker's reputation?

In Public

1. Are you impatient when you're not seated in a restaurant or attended to right away?
2. How do you react when you receive poor service at a restaurant or other business?
3. If a salesperson sold you a defective item that was expensive and refused to take it back, what would you do?
4. Do you give directions and recommendations on how to drive, what food to order, or what to buy when you're with others?
5. Do you hate waiting in lines and try to cut in front or bypass them altogether?
6. Have you ever gotten into a fight at a bar, restaurant, or party?
7. Are you chatty with strangers, or do you keep to yourself?
8. How do you feel about people who talk loudly or get drunk, rambunctious, flirtatious, or confrontational in public places?
9. How much of a tip do you usually leave when dining out?
10. Have you ever experienced road rage? If so, describe the situation.
11. What behaviors do you think are unacceptable in public (excluding those that are unlawful)?

Significant Others
Thoughts on Your Answers

In a well-known psychological experiment, adults were asked to point out the shortest of a group of lines on a poster. Every member of the group, except for one person, was secretly instructed to point to the longest line. When asked which line was shortest, one by one the members of the group pointed to the longest line. When it came time for the person who was not in on the secret to give his answer, he also chose the longer line although it was obviously incorrect. This experiment showed the sheer strength of peer pressure. People who are important in your lives have a tremendous influence on what you say and do. You may not be choosing lines in front of them, but you're just as concerned with their opinion.

When discussing your answers from the preceding chapters, talk about whether the following patterns were evident:

- **An overwhelming desire to please friends or relatives.** People who fear being disliked or disappointing others put the needs of others before their own, and their partner's as well. When choosing between helping a friend or helping their partner, the fearful person will help the friend. They worry about losing favor with their friends and overcompensate by bowing to their every desire.

- **Possessive or antisocial behavior.** If both of you consistently responded that you have no desire to spend time with the other's relatives or friends, you may find yourselves creating self-imposed isolation. A partner who says you're so good-looking that he can't trust you around other men is not being loving; he's being paranoid and possessive.

- **An inability to make the transition from single to married person.** Individuals who still see themselves as swinging singles or as children under their parent's care are living with an image incompatible with marriage. People who are very independent may be set in their solo lifestyle and find it very difficult to alter their schedule to include someone else. Although they love their partners and want to marry them, they don't want marriage to change their single lifestyle.

- **Unresolved feelings toward a past relationship.** Did you or your partner go into lengthy, sentimental descriptions about a past relationship, recalling exact dates and minute details? Such responses are commonly given by those unable to let go of a past love. Descriptions can be full of anger, confusion, fondness, or sadness. The former relationship may be long gone, but the time and energy spent thinking about it takes away from the time and energy that should be spent on your marriage.

An old Spanish saying states, "Show me your friends and I'll tell you who you are." As time goes by, your circle of friends changes. You'll add different coworkers, club members, neighbors, and parishioners to your social circle. While some friendships fade, others will evolve. Maintain friendships that enhance your relationship with your partner, but not ones that grow at its expense.

Part 4

Children

"Children have never been good at listening to their elders, but they have never failed to imitate them."

—James Baldwin

The decision whether or not to have children is without a doubt one of the most important decisions you will make in your life. Nothing will have a greater impact on your life than becoming a parent. Although many believe that having children and marriage go hand in hand, an increasing number of people believe it's a matter of choice. More inclined to see marriage as a partnership of two individuals, childless couples believe their talents and energies are better used in endeavors other than raising a family. Whether the reasons are ideological or medical, choosing not to have children is not a selfish act, but a selfless one. It's a great act of altruism when a couple realizes that, for them, it is best not to conceive.

If you choose to have children, you'll find few joys that surpass the feeling of raising a child together with your loving spouse. Children fill a home with laughter and happiness. Children, however, don't come with guarantees.

Having a child will not guarantee that you'll be taken care of in your old age. There are many abandoned elderly parents being cared for by public assistance, not their children.

Having a child does not guarantee that you'll never be alone. There are many parents who haven't seen their children in years.

Having a child does not guarantee that you'll get back all the love you felt you gave. Many parents and children are barely on speaking terms.

Children are created out of love and are given love unconditionally. Our only desire should be that they do the same when they have children of their own.

15

How Many, if Any?

Happily married couples can have different opinions on a variety of subjects. Childbearing and rearing should not be one of them. When raising children, you must think and act in unity. A child will find it difficult to follow instructions from parents who can't make decisions together.

Make sure you and your partner have discussed and *agreed on* the answers to all of the following questions.

1. Do you and your partner want to have children? If so, when do you plan to start a family?
2. How many children do you plan on having?
3. How many years would you like between the births of each child?
4. If you found out that you and your spouse could not conceive, would you (a) use fertility treatments, (b) use a sperm or egg donor, (c) become foster parents, (d) adopt, or (e) remain childless?
5. How important is it that you have at least one boy or one girl?
6. Would you continue to have children until you had at least one boy or girl?

7. If you've both decided *not* to have children, are you sure neither one will have a change of mind? What would happen if someone does change his or her mind?

8. As a woman, would you get pregnant without your partner's approval?

9. If you don't want to conceive, who will be responsible for birth control?

10. How disciplined are the two of you in consistently and correctly using birth control?

11. What backup form of birth control, if any, will you use?

12. What are your views on abortion? sterilization?

13. How will you and your spouse deal with an unplanned or unwanted pregnancy?

14. If your unborn child were diagnosed with a life-threatening disease, or a serious, but not lethal, deformity, would you continue with the pregnancy?

15. If the child your wife bore did not resemble you, would you be suspicious? Would you demand DNA testing?

16. Would you divorce your spouse if you could not bear children together?

17. How much time will you and your spouse agree to take off from your jobs once your child is born?

18. Will you and your partner be attending prenatal classes together?

19. Will your husband be in the delivery room to assist in the birth of your child?

20. Is having a child the single most important thing in your life?

Reasons to Conceive

The desire to have children can be strong. Desire, however, doesn't necessarily mean you're ready to start a family. The greatest gift you can give children is a stable and loving home where they can grow up seeing the beauty and compassion of a loving couple.

Create a list for each of the following topics.

List five reasons you would like to have children.

1. _____
2. _____
3. _____
4. _____
5. _____

List five reasons you would make a good parent.

1. _____
2. _____
3. _____
4. _____
5. _____

List five reasons your partner would make a good parent.

1. _____
2. _____
3. _____
4. _____
5. _____

List five things that worry you most about having children.

1. _____
2. _____
3. _____
4. _____
5. _____

Raising a Baby

Aside from being a full-time job, parenting requires that you and your spouse take on the roles of chefs, teachers, doctors, and taxi drivers. It may take a village to raise a child, but you and your spouse will be doing most of the work yourselves.

Answer the following questions with your partner. If your answers differ, decide on mutually acceptable answers to all of the following questions.

1. Who will get up to comfort and feed your crying baby during the night?
2. Who will take on the primary responsibility of disciplining your children?
3. Will your parenting style be similar to any of your parents, or someone else?
4. Do you believe children should be raised to fear and respect their elders and authority?
5. Will you strive to be your children's friend more than being a parental figure?
6. Describe your parenting style.

7. Have you ever said, "I want to give my kids everything I never had growing up"? If so, what was lacking in your childhood?

8. Do you want your children to have all the latest toys and games?

9. How do you feel about spanking a child?

10. Do you and your partner plan on being strict disciplinarians?

11. What priorities in life will you try to impress upon your children?

12. Describe how you would discipline your child for a minor offense. What do you consider a minor offense?

13. Describe a moderate and a serious offense and the corresponding disciplinary actions that you would take.

14. Describe the differences between discipline and child abuse.

15. Will you alter your TV viewing habits or language once you have children?

16. Will you, your spouse, and your children sleep in the same bed? If so, until your children reach what age?

17. Do you believe girls and boys should be raised differently? If so, how?

18. How much time do you plan on spending assisting your children with their schoolwork?

19. How important is it to you to teach manners to your children?

20. How will you show your children affection?

21. How would you feel about you or your spouse having a different last name than your children?

18

Financing a Family

The thought of a cute button nose and rosy little cheeks may make you forget that children cost money. Their food, clothes, toys, diapers, medicine, baby-sitters, and possibly day care will all become part of your regular household expenses.

Discuss the following questions with your partner. Be honest and realistic about how you plan to financially support a family.

1. Would you have a child without medical insurance coverage?
2. If you are waiting to have children until you feel you can afford them, what is enough money? If you didn't get to your monetary goal in an acceptable amount of time, how long would you continue waiting?
3. How would you manage to care for your child if he or she were born with a medical condition that required regular medical attention or hospitalization?
4. Are you and your partner aware of the costs of prenatal care?
5. Are you aware of the costs of diapers, formula, medicine, car seats, strollers, high chairs, cribs, and other infant care items?

6. Do you plan on saving money for your children's education or financial security? If not, how do you plan to pay for their education?

7. Will you go into debt to provide toys, clothes, a computer, or high-tech toys for your children?

8. Will your children be given an allowance? If "yes," what factors will influence the amount?

9. Do you and your spouse plan on sending your children to private school? If so, are you aware of the costs?

10. List the following in order of importance: your children, your marriage, personal happiness, the happiness of others, and financial stability.

11. Would you stay together in an unhappy marriage because of the financial security it offers your children?

12. To improve your child's quality of life would you (a) work multiple jobs or longer hours for more money or (b) work fewer hours or quit your job to spend more time with your child?

13. What are your feelings about nannies? day care?

14. How important is it that your child wears brand clothing?

15. Do you plan on enrolling your child in private lessons (music lessons, sports coaches, tutors, etc.)?

16. Will you and your spouse sacrifice purchases for yourselves to buy goods for your child?

17. Which would you choose: (a) a romantic vacation alone with your spouse or (b) a family vacation with your children?

18. If you could you live on one spouse's income, which one of you will be the stay-at-home parent?

19. Will you and your partner be able to afford day care if you both choose to work after your child is born?

20. Will one of you stay home until the child is old enough for that person to go back to work? What age do you consider old enough?
21. If a relative will be providing day care or baby-sitting your child, what will your options be if they can no longer provide this service?
22. Do you or your spouse plan on giving a cash inheritance to your children?

Stepchildren and Guardianship

For this exercise, "partner's children" will refer to any child or children *your partner* has from a previous relationship, while "my children" refers to any child or children *you* have from a previous relationship.

Working separately, answer each of the questions below. When finished, compare your answers. Check off questions where you and your partner's answers were in agreement.

	Yes	No	Answers Matched
I will be the primary caregiver of my partner's children.	○	○	○
My partner will be the primary caregiver of my children.	○	○	○
We agree on how much time our stepchildren will spend with us.	○	○	○
I am pursuing or will pursue full custody of my children from a previous relationship.	○	○	○
I support my partner's desire for full custody of his or her children.	○	○	○
I understand and accept the expenses incurred in raising my partner's children.	○	○	○

	Yes	No	Answers Matched
I do not want my partner's children involved in our life.	○	○	○
I do not want my children involved in my life with my future spouse.	○	○	○
I will favor children I have with my partner over those from a previous relationship.	○	○	○
I prefer that my children don't spend time with their other biological parent.	○	○	○
I prefer that my partner's children don't spend time with their other biological parent.	○	○	○
Contact with my partner's children will be limited to holidays or special events.	○	○	○
Contact with my children will be limited to holidays or other special events.	○	○	○
I completely trust my partner with my children.	○	○	○
I believe my partner's children are better off with his or her ex-partner or other guardian.	○	○	○
I believe my children are better off with my ex-partner or other guardian.	○	○	○
My partner and I will take our children from previous relationships on all of our vacations.	○	○	○
If any child from a previous relationship becomes too difficult to deal with, we will have them live with their other biological parent or their guardian.	○	○	○
I plan to legally adopt my partner's children.	○	○	○
My partner plans to legally adopt my children.	○	○	○

How Would You Respond?

Children are a never-ending source of amusement, warmth, inspiration, and wonder. They will challenge the way you see the world. You may feel that you learn more from them than they do from you. However, there will be other times when you'll ask, "Where in the world did they learn that?"

With your partner, answer the questions below. If the child's age is not specified, explain how your answers will differ depending on the age of the child.

How would you respond if . . .

1. your eight-year-old son came up to you and said, "I want to study ballet!"?
2. your spouse allowed your children to run around naked while company was visiting?
3. you found out your child shoplifted candy?
4. your child started using profanity?
5. your six-year-old had a tantrum at the supermarket checkout?
6. your twelve-year-old went out "tagging" (vandalizing property with graffiti) with his or her friends?
7. your son had no interest in sports?

8. your children wanted to eat junk food for breakfast, lunch, and dinner and screamed if you tried to feed them anything else?
9. your child was kicked out of school for being disruptive?
10. your pediatrician informed you that your son would only grow to be 5′4″ tall?
11. your daughter became a tomboy?
12. your child had an abnormally high IQ and could graduate high school by the age of nine?
13. your child kept skipping class?
14. your daughter was extremely beautiful and received a lot of attention from others?
15. your child was extremely shy?
16. your son was aggressive and frequently got into fights at school?
17. your child were overweight?
18. your child broke your neighbor's living room window?
19. your child said, "I hate you!"?
20. your child said, "You're the best mom (or dad) in the world?"
21. your child were eavesdropping on an argument you were having with each other?
22. your child wanted you to stop smoking, drinking, or coming home late from work?
23. your children hit each other or tried to hit you?
24. your children asked you about sex or your daughter wanted to go on birth control?
25. your child befriended another child whose mother you didn't like?
26. you were told your child had a learning disability and was doing poorly in school?

Children

Thoughts on Your Answers

Children can bring a sense of completion and purpose to your marriage. They are your living contribution to the world and a source of love and pride. However, not all couples choose to have children. This section may have opened your eyes to some of the overlooked aspects of having children and given you a realistic picture of the following:

- **How much you really enjoy children.** Do you only like infants, but have no patience with a sassy teenager? You can't choose to raise your child only during the "cute" years. Having children is a choice, not a requirement of marriage. Unless you and your partner are strongly committed to the idea and have an overwhelming desire to do so, perhaps you should wait to start a family until your feelings about the subject are more secure.

- **The kind of environment you and your partner will bring to your children.** Children learn to relate by seeing how you and your partner treat each other and those around you. Even as infants, they react to the tension of a stressed-out parent. Children belong in a home environment where a set schedule for feeding, sleeping, playing, and studying can be established. The answers you and your partner provided should describe the environment in which you plan to raise your family.

- **How in synch your parenting styles and expectations are.** If one of you believes in giving a child free reign of the house while the other is a strict disciplinarian, there's stormy weather ahead. By comparing your answers, you should be able to recognize whether you agree on the values you would like to pass on to your children.

- **The amount of time each one of you plans on spending with your children.** How much time you personally plan to spend with your children may be different from what your partner has in mind. You may be surprised to discover that your partner expected you to work full-time, whereas you assumed you'd be a stay-at-home parent. Naturally, all parents wants to maximize the amount of time they spend with their children. Yet, work obligations, social commitments, and other engagements prevent this from happening.

Review your answers in the preceding chapters. Who will be the one giving up the most of his or her personal time to care for the children? Will that partner do so willingly? Planning an even 50-50 division of responsibilities seems fair, but it's rarely achieved.

Part 5

Perspectives

"If we cannot end now our differences, at least we can help make the world safe for diversity."

—John Fitzgerald Kennedy

The attitudes and beliefs we have reveal our true identity, even more than where we came from, or what we choose to do for a living. You don't have to look too far into your past to see that your attitudes are dynamic. What you once believed to be true or most important may have changed or been reinforced over time.

Many individuals find that their attitude toward religion changes as they grow older or start a family. Some develop a strong desire to pass on religious beliefs and rituals to their children. Others reject or embrace spirituality during trying times. When discussing religious attitudes with your partner, ask yourself if your attitudes would remain the same if your surroundings were different.

Race is often not as important as a person's cultural identity. A child of Japanese parents who was born, educated, and raised in London, England, may identify more with British culture than that of Japan. Modern travel and communication allow people of the world to intermingle like never before. There is hardly a person or place remaining untouched by this cross-pollination of customs and traditions.

Your perspectives determine the path your future will take. They decide who will be your friends, how you relate to others at work, and what kind of example you will be presenting your children. Couples who share a vision of their future create a bond that will be strengthened as they progress toward this goal.

Religion and Spirituality

Couples who share the same religious beliefs may have an easier time enjoying a deep, spiritual bond and living their lives according to the teachings of their faith. Religious expression is an intimate and very personal aspect of one's identity, and there are many ways to express this faith.

Working separately, answer the questions below. When you finish, compare your answers. Discuss any discrepancies or areas of concern.

1. Do you and your partner share the same religious faith?
2. Is it important that your wedding be a religious ceremony?
3. How important is religion to your own life?
4. What are your own feelings about religion in general?
5. How often do you plan on attending religious services?
6. Will you attend regular religious services alone or with your partner?
7. Will you be an active member of your church's community?

8. Will you display religious symbols (crucifix, Star of David, etc.) in your home?

9. If you and your partner are of different religions, what, if any, conflicts could arise?

10. If you and your partner come from different religious backgrounds, in which faith (if any) will you raise your children?

11. Will you baptize your children in a faith you have no intention of practicing?

12. Do you harbor any negative feelings toward any particular religion or toward organized religion in general?

13. Will religion only play a part in your life during holidays or special occasions such as a bar mitzvah?

14. Will you contribute part of your income to a religious organization?

15. If you do not agree with your partner's religious views, will you discourage him or her from practicing the faith?

16. If a church service and a scheduled event, such as the Super Bowl or luncheon, were held at the same time, which would you attend?

17. Do you and your partner disagree about certain religious beliefs? If so, describe?

18. How would you react if your partner's religious convictions changed or followed a different direction after your marriage?

19. If you seek marital counseling, will you contact a religious professional such as a priest, pastor, or marriage counselor?

20. Do you believe religion's role is a source of comfort or stress?

21. Do you plan on converting to your partner's religion once you're married?

22. Do you believe marriage to be more a sacred or a legal union?
23. Are you a follower of mysticism or the occult?
24. Do you have a strong belief in astrology?
25. Do you plan your day based on your astrological forecast?
26. Do you believe God has a plan for you to follow? If so, what is it?
27. How strongly do you believe in fate and destiny?
28. Do you have a religious view of how the different sexes should behave?

Race and Culture

rban or rural, radical environmentalist or aggressive industrialist, culture isn't only relegated to issues of race or ethnicity. While some enjoy mingling with people with diverse ideas and ways of life, others choose to only socialize with those who closely resemble themselves. Our experiences with other races and cultures make us aware of our own racial and cultural identity, and our ability to accept others unlike ourselves.

With your partner, answer the questions below. Discuss your answers and how you both believe they could affect your marriage.

1. Do you or your partner avoid socializing with people of a different race or culture?
2. Do you or your partner believe that some racial or cultural stereotypes are true?
3. Have you or your partner ever discriminated against anyone based on race or culture?
4. Have you or your partner ever been the victim of racism?
5. Do you harbor any resentment or anger toward members of a particular racial or cultural group?
6. Will you teach your children to avoid socializing with others of a different race or culture?

7. What are your feelings toward racial or ethnic jokes and slurs?
8. If you're a culturally or racially mixed couple, how will you cope with those who don't approve of your union? How important is this to you, and how far would you go to change their minds?
9. Have you mostly been dated or been attracted to individuals of a race or culture different from your own?
10. If you're a culturally or racially mixed couple, do both sets of families support your relationship?
11. In general, what are your opinions about your partner's race or culture?
12. Do you and your partner maintain friendships with mixed couples or couples of different races than yours?
13. What is your biggest worry entering marriage as a mixed race/culture couple?
14. Do you believe your children will experience difficulties being of mixed race?
15. Do you believe your partner doesn't really understand or respect your culture? If so, what aspects?
16. Do you want to learn as much as you can about your partner's culture?
17. Will you encourage your partner to form friendships with members of his or her own race or culture?
18. Do you enjoy expressing your racial or cultural identity? If "yes," can you give examples?
19. Do you fear you're "disappointing" your race or ethnic group by marrying your partner?
20. Are you uncomfortable in a group where you are the only member of your race or culture? where your partner is the only member of his or her race or culture?
21. Do you fear your partner will leave you for a person of his or her own race or culture?

Politics

There have been several famous marriages in which the husband and the wife belong to opposing political parties. Despite their political differences, their relationships flourished. Although they are passionate about their political beliefs, they share the same desire to make their community a better place through government policies.

Discuss the following questions with your partner.

1. What's your political affiliation?
2. Do you think couples should share the same party affiliation?
3. Did you vote in the last election? If so, for which candidates?
4. What do you believe is the most important current issue in politics?
5. If you became a political activist, which organization would you support?
6. How would you feel if your partner supported an opposing candidate or political measure?
7. Are you politically conservative, moderate, or liberal?

8. Do you feel we have too little, too much, or just enough laws protecting the environment?
9. Have you ever participated in a demonstration? If so, describe the situation.
10. What cause would you support in a demonstration?
11. Do you consider yourself anti-establishment?
12. Do you believe there are political or special-interest groups that have too much power?
13. Do you believe politicians are more motivated by self-interest or serving the public?
14. What laws or policies do you think would make the world a better place?
15. Would you accept higher taxes in order to provide more services for the poor?
16. What are your views on illegal immigration?
17. If you were president, what percentage of the budget would you allocate to each of the following: education, conservation, defense, foreign aid, services for the elderly and poor?
18. Would you ever run for office?
19. Would you bribe or have you ever bribed a public official? Would you accept a bribe from a public official?
20. Do you feel it's important to get involved in your community?
21. Which laws would you repeal?
22. Describe a law that you would like to see passed.
23. What's your opinion on taxes? How would you determine who pays and how much should be paid?

Careers

So, what do you want to be when you grow up? You were often asked this question as a child. As an adult, are you asking yourself the same question? Some people define themselves by their professions. Others feel no attachment to their jobs and believe the only purpose of work is to provide a paycheck.

With your partner, answer the following questions.

1. Are you and your partner currently employed? If not, how long have you been unemployed?
2. Do you enjoy your job?
3. What is your ideal job?
4. If you have a degree, are you working in your field of your studies? If not, are you disappointed?
5. What kind of employee are you?
6. How long do you usually stay with a company?
7. If you owned a company, would you hire someone like yourself?
8. Have you ever lied to get a job or promotion?
9. Do you feel you have a "job," or a "career"?
10. Would you stay at a job you disliked just for the benefits?

11. Does your job require you to work weekends or holidays?
12. Would you take a job that required frequent overnight travel?
13. Would you work weekends or overtime even if you didn't receive additional pay?
14. If your child was performing in a school play, and your boss wanted you to put in overtime, would you stay at work or attend the play?
15. What's your opinion of mandatory employee drug testing?
16. Do you want to change careers? If so, what's your plan?
17. Would you rather have a job or be supported by your spouse?
18. How would you feel if your partner's job were more prestigious than yours?
19. Could you and your partner start a company together?
20. How would you feel if your partner were receiving raises and promotions, but you felt you were in a dead-end job?
21. How would you rate your job security? How often have you been unemployed?
22. Have you jumped from job to job looking for a career that satisfies you?
23. Are you proud of what you do for a living?
24. Are you proud of what your partner does for a living?
25. Would you support your spouse's dream of starting his or her own business or going back to school, even if it meant you needed to go back to work or that you wouldn't be financially stable for a while?
26. If you had your choice between a job that had average pay, but allowed you to spend evenings and weekends with your family, or a job that paid very well, but kept you away from your family on evenings and weekends, which would you choose?

27. Are you the type of person to take your work home with you?
28. Have you ever been called a workaholic?
29. Are you afraid of losing your job? If so, why?
30. What would you do if you or your partner were laid off and couldn't find work for over a year?

Seven Years Later

The saying "Be careful what you wish for because you might get it!" can also apply to mates. Traits that made you fall in love with your partner can turn into ones that drive you crazy a few years later.

Below are examples of how qualities initially perceived as good in a mate can turn sour later in the relationship. Discuss possible solutions, and if a similar situation could happen in your relationship.

Jenny was attracted to Jose because he was a hard worker and was moving up in his career.

Seven years later, she complains that he spends too much time at the office. Jose replies that he's always been serious about his job and she doesn't complain when he brings home his paycheck.

What would you advise this couple do to remedy their situation? Could something similar happen in your relationship?

Jack fell in love with Jan, a dancer at a trendy nightclub, the first time he laid eyes on her.

Seven years later, Jack gets angry at the thought of other men looking at his wife. Jan likes her job's hours and pay. In addition, she never said she would quit once they got married.

What would you advise this couple to do to remedy their situation? Could something similar happen in your relationship?

Rebecca married Ross because of his great sense of humor.

Seven years later, Rebecca is frustrated that Ross never takes anything seriously and is too busy clowning around to discuss important issues. Ross thinks Rebecca is far too uptight.

What would you advise this couple to do to remedy their situation? Could something similar happen in your relationship?

Dena is smitten by Don's big plans for the future.

Seven years later, Don is still planning, and Dena is the only one working to pay the bills. Don tells her to be patient.

What would you advise this couple to do to remedy their situation? Could something similar happen in your relationship?

Colette's laid-back style was just what Carl was looking for to offset his own hectic lifestyle.

Seven years later, Carl accuses Colette of being a couch potato with no ambition. Colette responds by telling Carl that he stresses himself out for no good reason, and being a rat in the rat race is not her style.

What would you advise this couple to do to remedy their situation? Could something similar happen in your relationship?

Ed was impressed at how good Emily always looked.

Seven years later, Ed demands that Emily stop spending so much money on clothes and beauty treatments. Emily claims it costs money to look beautiful.

What would you advise this couple to do to remedy their situation? Could something similar happen in your relationship?

Beth was excited by Brian's mysterious bad-boy image.

Seven years later, Beth complains that Brian hangs around people she doesn't trust, and that he's absent for most of the day without giving any indication of his whereabouts. Brian feels that Beth is placing too many demands on him.

What would you advise this couple to do to remedy their situation? Could something similar happen in your relationship?

Keith was drawn to Keri's assertive style and bold attitude.

Seven years later, Keith accuses Keri of being bossy and overbearing. Keri states she's just strong willed and should fight for what she thinks is right.

What would you advise this couple to do to remedy their situation? Could something similar happen in your relationship?

Sam loved all the attention Susan gave him. Her frequent calls made him feel loved.

Seven years later, Sam feels smothered by Susan's constant questions about where he's been, whom he's seen, and what he's been doing. Susan replies that she's just curious about his daily life.

What would you advise this couple to do to remedy their situation? Could something similar happen in your relationship?

Your Future

When describing your future at various milestones in your relationship, ask yourselves if you and your partner share a common goal for your future.

With your partner, describe yourselves at the following stages of your marriage.

One-Year Anniversary

Place of residence:
Type of housing:
Profession and income:
Family size:
Describe a typical week in your life:

Ten-Year Anniversary

Place of residence:
Type of housing:
Profession and income:
Family size:
Describe a typical week in your life:

Twenty-Year Anniversary

Place of residence:
Type of housing:
Profession and income:
Family size:
Describe a typical week in your life:

Thirty-Year Anniversary

Place of residence:
Type of housing:
Profession and income:
Family size:
Describe a typical week in your life:

Forty-Year Anniversary

Place of residence:
Type of housing:
Profession and income:
Family size:
Describe a typical week in your life:

Fifty-Year Anniversary

Place of residence:
Type of housing:
Profession and income:
Family size:
Describe a typical week in your life:

Perspectives
Thoughts on Your Answers

When you're in love, the world takes on a more beautiful appearance. Love songs you once thought were corny now ring true. Even a partner's dirty socks can provoke a romantic sigh. Nothing can be wrong about something that feels so wonderful. Some lovers get so caught up in the euphoria of being engaged that they float from cloud to cloud, oblivious to everything around them. Some are so convinced that their partner is "the one" that they reject any possibility that there might be trouble in wonderland. Love may conquer all, but it cannot offset opposing fundamental beliefs held by you and your partner. The questions in the preceding chapters should have helped you realize:

- **What you can give up and what you will not.** A close friend recalls how she was willing to convert to Judaism for her boyfriend when the relationship became serious. The more she thought about it, the more she came to realize that her Christianity was not only a strong force in her culture, but also a part of her life that she enjoyed practicing and would never feel comfortable abandoning. Today you may not mind compromising certain areas of your life, but could you continue to do so for the rest of your life?

- **Which differences will keep your relationship fresh and interesting and which will pull you apart.** You get a big kick watching your partner load up on the Tabasco while you enjoy steamed rice and unsalted, blanched carrots. Idiosyncrasies between partners keep a relationship interesting. But if differences extend past food preferences and into personal philosophies about life, you may have a problem. Opposing views on condiments are superficial. Opposing views on cultural traditions are significant.

- **If you're underplaying differences in order to make the relationship work.** Getting to the altar and saying "I do" should not be a goal in itself. If you find yourself brushing aside disagreements or avoiding discussions about a variety of subjects, you may be repressing serious issues that need to be addressed before becoming husband and wife.

- **How knowledgeable you are about what's important to you.** Your partner may enthusiastically assume the risks, unstable pay, and long hours it takes to start his or her own business. However, you may believe it's more important to have a steady paycheck and free weekends together. Getting married is a lifetime decision; it can hardly be made when you haven't decided what you want from life.

Opposites do attract, but it's what you have in common that makes a successful marriage. Hollywood loves pairing mismatched couples and having them ride off into the sunset in wedded bliss. The shoe may have fit Cinderella, but if fondness for footwear is the only thing she and her prince shared, then the marriage will most likely meet the same fate as her magic carriage.

Part **6**

Daily Life and Lifestyles

> "Happiness doesn't come from doing what we like to
> do but from liking what we have to do."
>
> —Wilfred Peterson

Dividing household duties is what domestic teamwork is all about. Yet, something so simple as making a pot of coffee can explode into a battle of the sexes. As far as household duties go, there is no such thing as "men's work" or "women's work."

For those seeking perfect equality in the household, there really is no way to equally divide the work. The best one can hope for is to "acceptably" divide the chores, in other words, divide duties in a way that is acceptable to both spouses. For example, one person may agree to do all the household chores as long as he or she never has to do a single load of laundry. The division of labor may not be equal, but for that person, the thought of never having to fluff and fold more than makes up for the discrepancy.

Discrepancies can also show up in how a couple chooses to spend their leisure time. Rest and relaxation can mean a day of fishing for one person, and a day of shopping for the other. Every person needs to set some time aside to unwind. Although you may not agree with how your partner chooses to do so, respect his or her right to relieve stress. Couples should allow each other a moment of uninterrupted calm, whether it is achieved together or alone.

Who Will Do What?

Deciding who will do which specific chores can sometimes degenerate into a battle of wills. Dividing up the work ahead of time can help in preventing future arguments.

Working separately, answer the questions below. When you are finished, compare answers.

Task	Who?	How Often?	How Important?
Washing dishes			
Vacuuming			
Dusting			
Tidying up at the end of the day			
Making the bed			
Grocery shopping			
Going to the drug store			
Picking up and going through the mail			
Replying to invitations			
Cleaning the house or apartment			
Doing yard work			
Decorating your home			
Doing the laundry and putting it away			
Selecting the movies			

Task	Who?	How Often?	How Important?
Driving your children to their various appointments			
Driving your children to day care or school			
Shopping for clothes			
Calling the doctor, mechanic, or other professionals for an appointment			
Staying home and waiting for repair, installation, or delivery personnel			
Deciding what you watch on TV (if you share a TV)?			
Washing the car			
Doing minor household repairs and maintenance (unclogging toilet, fixing leaky faucet)			
Doing minor auto repairs and maintenance			
Taking out the trash			
Making the morning coffee			
Picking up clothes from the cleaners			
Call for estimates or comparison shop for goods and services			
Investigating and resolving billing disputes			

Daily Routine

A movie realistically depicting the lives of couples in long-lasting and happy marriages would have you snoozing in your seat. It would feature yawn-inspiring scenes of couples paying bills, going to the supermarket, and watching television. Hollywood leads us to believe that you must have trauma and drama to experience true love. This is not the case. Strong relationships are built by participating in daily routines together.

With your partner, answer and discuss the questions below.

1. Do you have a daily routine? If so, what is it?
2. How will your daily routine change once you're married?
3. What part of your daily routine do you refuse to change once you're married?
4. Is there any aspect of your partner's daily routine that bothers you?
5. How do you feel when someone monopolizes the TV remote control?
6. Do you or will you have a favorite chair that only you can use?
7. How often do you bathe? brush your teeth?
8. How often do you shave?

9. How do you feel when you come home after a difficult day at work?
10. What's the first thing you do when you come home after work?
11. Do you consider yourself a morning person or a night person?
12. Realistically, do you expect your home to always look neat and clean, or messy but not disgustingly dirty?
13. Do you need to take naps or sleep in on a regular basis?
14. Do you prefer to keep the radio or TV on all day, even if you're not home?
15. Are you a busybody?
16. Do you like reading or watching TV in bed?
17. Do you leave clothes or shoes lying around?
18. What do you believe is a comfortable room temperature?
19. Do you often forget to do household chores, or put them off as much as possible?
20. Which household chores do you like the least?
21. Is there a regularly scheduled TV program that you follow and don't want to miss?

Changes

When a person receives a promotion, job duties and priorities change. Marriage is somewhat like a career promotion. There will be changes in your responsibilities and what is expected. It would be foolish to accept a job or enter a marriage without being aware of the changes this new role will bring.

Working on separate copies, place a check mark in the circle that represents the level of change you expect once you marry. When you are finished, discuss your answers.

	Stay the Same	Get Better	Get Worse	Neither Better Nor Worse— Just Different
Our sex life	○	○	○	○
Our finances	○	○	○	○
Availability of leisure time	○	○	○	○
Our social life	○	○	○	○
Household furniture	○	○	○	○
Style and frequency of vacations	○	○	○	○
Time spent with close friends	○	○	○	○
Relationship with each other	○	○	○	○
Relationship with our parents	○	○	○	○
Relationship with our in-laws	○	○	○	○
Physical appearance	○	○	○	○

	Stay the Same	Get Better	Get Worse	Neither Better Nor Worse— Just Different
Frequency of dining out	○	○	○	○
Housing	○	○	○	○
Combined credit rating	○	○	○	○
Television viewing habits	○	○	○	○
Individual stress load	○	○	○	○
Enjoyment of our jobs	○	○	○	○
Career ambitions	○	○	○	○
Tolerance for your partner's quirks	○	○	○	○
Social outings without your partner	○	○	○	○

Do You Mind?

Socks on the floor, an empty milk carton in the refrigerator, wet towels on the bed—all examples of little things that go unnoticed by one person, but make another's hair stand on end. Everybody has a list of pet peeves, and it's almost guaranteed that your partner will do at least one of the items on your list. Likewise, you've probably mastered one on your partner's list as well.

Working separately, you and your partner are to make lists of your top ten annoyances. Would anything listed below make it on your list?

Hair in the sink
Toothpaste in the sink
Wet towels on the floor or bed
Sound of cracking knuckles
Receiving driving instructions from a passenger
Channel surfing on the TV
Talking with mouth full of food
Setting a glass on a table without using a coaster
Opening mail addressed to someone else
Interrupting someone telling a story
Empty beverage containers in refrigerator

Nail biting
Someone reading while you speak to them
Someone speaking to you when you're trying to read
Using baby talk with adults
Clutter
Dirty dishes in the sink overnight
Visible dust on the furniture
People telling the punch line of a joke they didn't start
Hearing or seeing someone chew gum
Someone wearing a hat indoors
Not receiving a thank-you card
Arriving late (you or others)
Not returning phone calls
Others criticizing things you support (religion, politics, sports)
Dinner not being ready when you get home from work
Watching TV while eating a meal
TV in the bedroom
Eating in a room other than the kitchen or dining room
Phone calls during dinner
Dirty or untrimmed fingernails
Nail clippings on the floor
Whistling
Singing with the radio
Putting feet on the furniture
Unflushed toilets
Leaving the cap off the toothpaste
Leaving jar lids loose
Leaving the toilet seat up

Daily Life and Lifestyles
Thoughts on Your Answers

Your marriage is about your average day, not your wedding day. It is made up of the day-to-day, tedious activities spiced up with occasional drama and humorous events. It's surprising to find that brides and grooms spend more time agonizing over which flowers to use at their wedding than discussing what duties each will assume to run a happy and efficient home. The compatibility we have with our partner is never more evident than in the way ordinary events are transformed into a touching occasion merely by the fact that you are doing it together.

It may seem trivial to discuss who will cook and who will wash the dishes, but these questions are important because:

- **Small things add up.** It's an unfortunate reality that a subject so simple as taking out the trash can start some couples down a path of irreversible damage. Infidelity, separation, and even divorce are rarely due to an isolated disagreement. They are caused by an accumulation of little resentments and unresolved disagreements. If the previous chapters have suggested that you and your partner have different ideas about how you'll be spending your free time, or divide the household responsibilities, then time must be taken to find a resolution to these differences.

- **You need to clarify which duties you'll each be responsible for.** Individuals working together as a unit achieve success in the military. Each soldier knows his or her own tasks and responsibilities, as well as those of colleagues as they join forces to ensure victory. Couples that adopt this strategy go through life like a well-oiled machine. They are clear on the mission and how it should be accomplished. Without this focus, you'll find bickering and uncertainty, with more time spent arguing over tasks than actually getting them done.

- **A good spouse can be a lousy roommate.** Discuss how each of you will approach and carry out this daily routine while living together. By doing so, you'll begin to see how compatible you are, not as parents or lovers, but as roommates. You may see eye to eye on every subject such as religion, parenting methods, and finances, but will it drive you crazy that your spouse is an incurable slob? Or that he or she prefers to spend every weekend on the sofa watching television?

A wedding is one day, your marriage is for the rest of your life. In time you and your partner will discover habits that drive each other crazy. The questions in the previous chapters give you a chance to discuss these behaviors and decide if the positive qualities you each posses outweigh your less desirable idiosyncrasies.

Part 7

Leisure Time

"Leisure unmasks our weaknesses."

—Mason Cooley

Your leisure time will be taken up by a combination of pleasurable and practical activities. Your practical activities will consist of household errands, maintenance work, or family obligations. Your pleasurable activities may include outings with your children, sports, outdoor activities, hobbies, and travel.

As time progresses, you'll notice a change in how you travel and spend your leisure time at home. Honeymoon-style vacations will give way to family-friendly trips. Nights out on the town will be replaced by quiet dinners at home. These changes occur not because you've been *forced* to stay home, but because you *prefer* to stay home.

Either way, you will have many opportunities to create memorable moments of the time you share together.

How You Relax

Leisure time is the time remaining once you've deducted hours spent sleeping and working. But how leisurely you spend these remaining hours is purely a matter of choice.

Working separately, fill in the table below. Under the column "How often?" enter *D* for daily, *W* for weekly or on weekends, *O* for occasionally, and *Y* for activities you plan on doing once or twice a year.

Activity	Details what kind, where, and with whom	How Often?	For How Long at a Time?
Shopping			
Doing chores			
Running errands			
Gardening			
Watching TV			
Browsing Internet sites			
Visiting chat rooms			
Talking on the phone			
Working on a hobby			
Going out for breakfast			
Going out for lunch			

Activity	Details *what kind, where, and with whom*	How Often?	For How Long at a Time?
Going out for dinner			
Going out for drinks or drinking at home			
Having company over			
Going to concerts			
Going to fairs or community events			
Gambling			
Attending sporting events			
Doing volunteer work			
Participating in outdoor recreational activity			
Exercising			
Working out at a gym			
Playing video or com- puter games			
Watching movies			
Participating in recre- ational activities with your children			
Playing a sport			
Attending or teaching classes			
Doing home repairs and maintenance			
Attending seminars or workshops			
Other (list separately)			

Planning a Trip

Traveling together combines several stressful situations—dealing with unfamiliar rooms, restaurants, roads, and directions—and concentrates them into a short time designated as to be a time to relax. How well you plan a trip can also add to (or subtract from) the stress that normally accompanies travel.

Working with your partner, answer the questions below to determine each other's travel style.

1. Do you prefer to arrive at airports or train stations well ahead of schedule or minutes before departure?
2. Do you create an itinerary for your trips? If so, how detailed are they, and do you mind getting off schedule?
3. Do you create a budget for your trips? If so, how detailed are they and do you usually come in over, under, or right on budget?
4. Do you prefer unstructured, come-what-may itineraries?
5. Do you prefer to travel on your own, or on a guided tour with others?
6. When you travel, do you prefer to stay in hotels, with friends, or with relatives?
7. Do you only fly first class?

8. Are there any parts of the world you won't visit?
9. Do you prefer to vacation domestically or abroad?
10. Which would you choose: a vacation in the great outdoors, a luxury cruise, or sightseeing in a large American city?
11. Are you a light or a heavy packer?
12. How would you describe your perfect vacation?
13. How would you describe a luxury vacation? Have you ever taken one? If so, what did you like about the experience? dislike?
14. How would you describe a midlevel vacation? Have you ever taken one? If so, what did you like about the experience? dislike?
15. How would you describe a budget vacation? Have you ever taken one? If so, what did you like about the experience? dislike?
16. Which of the following would you feel uncomfortable taking: a budget, a midlevel, or a luxury vacation?
17. Do you like planning your vacations months or just a few weeks ahead of time?
18. Do you prefer to take fewer but longer vacations or those that are shorter but more frequent?
19. Do you enjoy camping or long trips by car?
20. Have you ever had a horrible vacation experience? If so, describe.

33

Your Traveling Style

You can find a multitude of travel guides to help you find your way around any part of the world. What's missing from these guides is how to navigate the potential rough waters of traveling with your partner. Traveling together offers a unique opportunity to highlight our reactions to crisis and to show what activities we seek for amusement.

Working separately, answer the questions below. When you are finished, compare your answers with your partner's and discuss.

1. Do you like to go to bed and wake up early or go to bed late and sleep in the next day?
2. If you and your partner forgot your airline tickets and couldn't board your flight, or your hotel couldn't find your reservation, what would you do?
3. When traveling, do you typically eat at restaurants, order room service, or eat at the homes of friends or relatives?
4. If you typically eat in restaurants, could you describe the types of places where you would eat breakfast, lunch, snacks, and dinner?

5. Will you avoid small, locally owned restaurants, especially if traveling in a foreign country?
6. When traveling together by car, who will drive and who will read the map?
7. What are your thoughts on separate vacations? Would you and your partner ever take them? If so, under what conditions?
8. Would you attend a time-share or other sales presentation?
9. Would you ever purchase a time-share or invest in real estate or a business on vacation?
10. Would you pay a friend's or relative's expenses to have that person travel with you?
11. What types of souvenirs do you buy? How many do you buy, and how much do you spend on them?
12. Would you and your partner be willing to share a hotel room with friends or relatives?
13. Who will most likely take the lead in deciding when and where to go once you've arrived at your location?
14. Do you insist on room upgrades, views, more towels, or other nonstandard items at a hotel?
15. Have you ever gotten lost while traveling? How did (or would) you react?
16. When touring an area, how long do you sightsee between meals or stops to rest?
17. How much of your vacation time do you spend shopping, relaxing in your hotel room, and visiting cultural sights?
18. How do you react when planes, trains, or fellow travelers (including your partner) are late?
19. How long does it take you to get ready to go out?
20. Do you take items from your hotel room?

21. Describe what type of guest you are when staying at the home of a friend or relative.

22. If you decide to stay with a friend or relative while traveling, how do you show your appreciation for their hospitality?

Are We Having
Fun Yet?

Henry Higgins sang of the misery of letting a woman into his life of leisure. Lucy Ricardo showed us the mishaps that can happen while on vacation, and Madam Bovary demonstrated the danger of having too much time on one's hands. Your free time can get you into circumstances that weren't expected.

With your partner, answer the questions below and come up with a solution to each situation.

1. It's a beautiful day outside. Your partner wants to stay home and watch television. You want her to accompany you to a local park. What would you do? What if the tables were turned and you didn't want to go outdoors?
2. You've been going to the same restaurant every week-end. You like the food and knowing what to expect when it's served. Your partner wants a change and insists on going elsewhere. What would you do? What if the tables were turned and you didn't want to go to the same restaurant?

3. You're on vacation at a beach resort. While your partner is getting refreshments, you spot a beach babe making friendly conversation with him. What would you do? What if a beach hunk came up to you and started making friendly conversation?

4. While staying at your parents' house over the weekend, your partner wants to make love, but you're afraid your parents will hear you. What would you do? What would you do if you were feeling frisky and were staying at your in-laws' house?

5. Your partner promised to fix the leaky faucet over the weekend. But, when the weekend arrived, he spent it playing golf and video games. What would you do? Have you ever broken a promise to do something around the house?

6. You're taking a two-day road trip. Your partner frequently needs to use a restroom but will only use those in hotel lobbies. This is inconvenient and time-consuming. What would you do? What if you were the one that would only visit selected restrooms?

7. You want to go dancing, but your partner has no interest. You feel uncomfortable going stag with other couples, and neither of you thinks you should go alone. What would you do? What if your partner wanted to go to a club you had no interest in visiting?

8. The weekend arrives, and your partner tells you she's bored. You, on the other hand, have plenty to do, but they're tasks that don't need assistance. What would you do? What if you were the one who was bored while your partner was busy?

9. You're looking forward to a quiet weekend at home reading a good book. Your partner surprises you with

news that he's invited ten people over for a barbecue. What would you do? What if you wanted to invite people over, but your partner didn't want to entertain company?

10. You have four days of vacation, but only two days of money left. What would you do?

Leisure Time
Thoughts on Your Answers

People are working longer hours and taking fewer holidays than in the past. Leisure time has become a short time span in which you try to squeeze in errands, family outings, and maybe a little time for yourself.

If you haven't lived together before marriage, be prepared for having your partner around during most of your free time. On the positive side, you can divide the work of household chores. Plus, having less time alone is, for many, a selling point of marriage. Yet, for those who live very independently or spend their leisure time doing solitary projects, sharing their personal time may take some getting use to.

Unlike other areas of your marriage such as raising a family or sexual intimacy, your preferred recreational activities can be completely different and still not pose any problems in your relationship. You may squabble a bit, but you probably won't want to divorce your partner because she didn't enjoy hiking the Grand Canyon.

Because your leisure time is so limited, make an effort to take advantage of every minute. The following suggestions can help you maximize the fun and minimize your stress:

- **Don't try to cram one week of errands into one weekend.** If you return to work more exhausted than when you left, you're probably trying to do too much in too little time. Spread your errands out over the week and drop those that are more busy-work than necessities. If possible, pay a little more for services that free up your time. Your home should be a place to relax, not a hard labor camp.

- **Schedule some "couple time."** Make sure you have some time set aside when you can relax and reconnect with your partner. Set aside a few hours, or even thirty minutes. Turn off the TV, put the kids to bed or have them take a nap, and spend some quality time alone. Making this a fixed part of your routine will be immensely rewarding.

- **Don't feel you have to do all your activities with each other.** Having shared interests keeps you together. Having different ones keeps you interesting. Try to have a combination of both. Your partner didn't fall in love with you because you're his or her mirror image. Exercise your own thoughts by reading, taking classes, or participating in other activities on your own. It will nourish your mind and make you more engaging.

- **Set up some ground rules before going on vacation.** Some couples take vacations together with ease; others do so with disastrous results. Unless you both have mastered the art of diplomacy or have dozens of trips together under your belt, decide who will be the person to take the lead in making decisions. You don't have to relinquish total control. You can trade off being leaders on different days. Democracy doesn't work well when you want to take the road on your left, and your partner wants to take the one to the right.

Although leisure time is when you get to relax and do as you please, be courteous when traveling or staying at home. Respect the rules and the property of others. Don't be the visitor who is not welcomed back, or the type of roommate that drives your partner crazy.

Part 8

Finances

"There are people who have money, and people
who are rich."

—Coco Chanel

Research shows that the subject couples argue about most is money. Spouses frequently disagree on how to best manage the family finances, regardless of whether the couple is rich or poor. Arguments often erupt over who paid for what, how much it cost, and whether the purchase was even necessary. It isn't long before accusations of being cheap or financially irresponsible are tossed back and forth, and real problems come to the surface. When they disagree about money issues, couples don't always argue. Instead, they often hide information from each other. Studies reveal that a spouse is more likely to withhold information regarding a financial affair than an extramarital one.

Couples may talk endlessly about their dream home and future together, but they rarely talk about how they intend on financing these dreams. Talking about finances while dating can feel very awkward—not to mention unromantic. The subject is often avoided, and each person assumes that when it comes to money, "What's mine is mine, and what's yours is yours." But once a couple marries, the "mine" quickly becomes "ours," as bank accounts and financial responsibilities merge.

Of all the major elements that affect your marriage, finance is the area in which you have the most control.

Saving and Spending Styles

What determines how much you'll spend at the grocery store? For a new car? Or a new coat? When talking about money, we usually limit ourselves to two topics: what we (or others) have, and what we (or others) spend. However, a third topic needs to be discussed—the emotional connections to money. When we understand what motivates us to save and spend, we can become better money managers.

With your partner, ask each other the questions below and discuss your answers.

Your Saving Style

1. What motivates you to save money?
2. Does saving money make you feel good or deprived?
3. If you were given $3,000 in cash, would you save it or spend it?
4. How concerned are you about saving for retirement?
5. Do you have money set aside for a "rainy day" or an emergency fund in case you lose your source of income?

6. Given a choice between saving and spending, which do you usually choose?
7. Do you actively seek out sales and bargains or clip coupons?
8. How familiar are you with the various types of available financial investments such as stocks, bonds, 401(k)s, and IRAs.
9. Does part of your paycheck go directly to one of your company's investment plans such as 401(k), stock purchase program, or credit union?
10. Do you find it easy or difficult to save money?
11. Do you save up enough cash for large purchases such as furniture, appliances, and vacations, or do you use credit cards and carry the balance?
12. Do you have a secret stash of money set aside?
13. Do you understand the concept of compound interest?
14. Are you always thinking of ways to save money?
15. Have you ever been accused of being a cheapskate?
16. Are your attitudes toward saving money based on childhood experiences?

Your Spending Style

1. Are you an impulsive spender?
2. Do you have an expensive hobby?
3. What motivates you to spend money?
4. Do you ever get buyer's remorse or frequently fear that you've paid too much for an item?
5. Are you a regular gambler?
6. How much debt are you currently carrying, excluding a mortgage?
7. Do you have a current copy of your credit report, or do you know your current credit rating?
8. Have you ever bounced a check?

9. Do you purchase clothes or other items that you never end up using?
10. Are you in credit card debt for designer clothes and accessories?
11. How much do you usually spend on a gift for a friend or relative?
12. Have you ever been called a spendthrift or "shopaholic"?
13. Do you purchase items to "keep up with the Joneses"?
14. Are you indifferent about carrying a large amount of personal debt?
15. Do you enjoy purchasing gifts for other people?
16. Do you get a "rush" or sense of power when making a sizeable purchase?

Managing Your Money

Since the advent of credit, people are no longer limited to making purchases purely based on how much cash they have on hand. This has turned out to be a mixed blessing. While it enables people to buy homes and automobiles, it also enables them to overspend until bankrupt.

Who will be responsible for . . .

1. making sure the bills get paid on time?
2. determining the monthly budget?
3. deciding how many credit cards you each can have?
4. deciding how much debt you can carry on each card?
5. keeping financial receipts and documents?
6. preparing your taxes?
7. balancing your checkbooks and other financial statements?
8. choosing a bank or financial institution?
9. making investment decisions?
10. negotiating financial contracts such as leases or loan agreements?

How would you feel if . . .

1. your partner forbade you from purchasing an item, such as a big-screen TV or an expensive pair of shoes?
2. your partner wanted to quit his or her job and go back to school, making you the only source of income for your family?
3. your partner managed all your money or made all the major financial decisions?
4. you received a gift of money from your relatives? Would you keep it for yourself or share it with your partner?
5. you or your partner was the only one bringing home an income?
6. your partner bought an expensive item without consulting you first?
7. your partner had a higher income than you did?
8. your partner wanted to accept a lower-paying job or turned down a promotion?
9. you or your partner lost a sizeable amount of money in a bad investment?
10. you found out your partner was hiding money from you?
11. your partner loaned someone money without your approval?

When Times Get Tough

Almost every couple experiences a period during their marriage when household expenses need to be reduced. This financial downsizing could be the result of a job loss or a plan to save money for a large purchase or investment. Whatever the reasons, unless a couple works together as a team, the chance of reaching their financial goal is slim.

The list below represents regular expenses incurred within one year. Suddenly, you must drastically cut your spending. Working separately, cross out items to be eliminated and circle expenditures you can't live without. When finished, compare answers and come up with a single list of only five shared expenses.

Lawn and garden service
Housekeeper or cleaning service
Day care or nanny
Serviced car wash
Expensive haircuts or hair treatments
Beauty treatments (manicures, waxing, etc.)
Massages or chiropractic care
Purchases of clothes or shoes
Dry cleaning

Cable TV
A second car
Full-coverage auto insurance
Out-of-town vacations
Going out to movies
Concerts or professional sporting events
Dining out
Ordering take-out meals or fast food
Buying snacks or other nonessential food items
Daily stops at a specialty coffee shop
Buying lunch at work
Weekly outings with friends
Birthday gifts for friends
Having and maintaining a pet or pets
Club membership dues or expenses
Gym membership or personal trainer
Paying more than the minimum due on monthly bills
Rented storage space
Visiting amusement parks or other attractions
Contributions to charity or parish
Expenses incurred by a hobby
Alcoholic beverages
Cigarettes or cigars
Child's private schooling, lessons, or tutors
Schooling or classes taken by you or your spouse
Home repair projects
Lottery tickets or other gaming activities
Sending or loaning money to relatives
Internet access charges
Magazine and newspaper subscriptions
Cell phones or pagers
Saving for retirement (401(k), IRA, or other)
Contributions towards a college savings fund

Money Honesty

A recent poll discovered that the most common deception among married individuals involved money. Couples should always be open about money matters. Each person needs to be completely clear on what money is individually owned and free to be saved or spent at each person's own discretion, versus what money is to be used for shared purposes.

With your partner, read each scenario out loud. Choose the option that best describes how each of you would handle the given situation.

1. Your partner asks for money for half of the phone bill, which is now due. You have the money, but you're saving it to spend over the weekend. You
   a. say you don't have a dime.
   b. give him or her the money to pay your share of the phone bill.
   c. get angry over how the bills seem to be getting out of control.
   d. wait until next month's paycheck to pay the bill plus any overdue charges.

2. You're having drinks with friends you haven't seen in a while. The check arrives. You
   a. say, "This round's on me!"
   b. calculate each person's tab, including tax and tip.
   c. leave before anyone asks for money.
   d. divide the bill equally by the number of people at the table.
3. An expensive item you've been dying to own has just been reduced in price. You and your partner have agreed to cut your spending, but this is an irresistible purchase. You
   a. purchase the item and hide it, or tell your partner it was a gift.
   b. resist the temptation to buy the item.
   c. buy it with money borrowed from a friend or relative.
   d. work overtime, do odd jobs, or sell some belongings to come up with the cash.
4. A coworker is taking up a collection to purchase a going-away gift for another coworker whom you know, but are not close to. You're on a very limited budget. You
   a. say you can only donate five bucks.
   b. say you will get the person a gift on your own, but never do so.
   c. decline giving money, but say you'd like to sign the card.
   d. contribute the same amount as everyone else, even if it's over your limit.
5. An organization for a cause you believe in, but your partner does not, is requesting donations. You
   a. donate without hesitation, since it's your own money.
   b. discuss with your partner the intended donation before handing over any money.

    c. forgo donating the money, but offer your time instead.

    d. find a charity you both agree to support, and make a contribution in both your names.

6. Your back has been bothering you, but you're unsure of the cause. You

    a. take a vacation, since it's probably stress related.

    b. view the injury as an opportunity to sue someone and hopefully make a few bucks.

    c. file for disability payments and try to convince a doctor the pain is work related.

    d. seek medical attention that doesn't get in the way of your work schedule.

7. Your high school reunion is coming up. You're not as financially successful as you would like. You

    a. go and have a great time. This is a reunion, not a salary contest.

    b. don't go.

    c. rent an expensive car, borrow an expensive outfit, and lie about your profession at the party.

    d. go, but exaggerate how well you are doing.

8. You and your partner have been asked to dine with friends at a very expensive restaurant you really can't afford. You

    a. tell the couple you'd love to dine with them at a less-expensive restaurant.

    b. tell the couple thanks, but you have other plans for that evening.

    c. bite the bullet and go since that's what credit cards are for.

    d. decline, feeling offended. Only snobs choose expensive restaurants to show off.

9. When preparing your taxes, you
    a. give full disclosure and 100 percent accurate information.
    b. pad an expense here and there.
    c. don't file tax returns because you believe they're unfair.
    d. make up dependents or business expenses.

Our First Budget

There is no better way to find out your financial standing than to compare how much you make to how much you spend and owe. The worksheet below will help you determine if your combined incomes can support your household expenses. It's the first step in financial planning. Next is defining which expenses will be shared and which will be paid individually. This second step may seem inconsequential, but it provides an opportunity to correct any misconceptions about how much each of you expects to contribute to a given expense.

Fill in your expected monthly income and expenditures in the worksheet below. For expenditures that vary from month to month (such as gifts), take the total you spent the previous year and divide by 12. Next, enter who will pay the expense. If the answer is "both," discuss whether the expense will be evenly divided, or if one person will pay a larger share.

Your Expected Net Income *(Total take-home pay)*	$	Who Will Pay?		
		Your		
Expenses	$	You	Partner	Both
Rent or mortgage		○	○	○
Renter's/homeowner's insurance		○	○	○
Car payments		○	○	○

Expenses	$	Who Will Pay?		
		You	Your Partner	Both
Auto insurance		○	○	○
Gasoline		○	○	○
Other auto expenses (parking, washing, repairs, etc.)		○	○	○
Debt payments (student, home equity, or other loans)		○	○	○
Consumer debt (credit card payments or other financed purchases)		○	○	○
Utilities (gas, electricity, water, other power sources)		○	○	○
Phones/pagers (includes land and cell phones)		○	○	○
Savings or investment contributions		○	○	○
Cable TV		○	○	○
Internet expenses (high-speed access and subscription fees)		○	○	○
Lunches and dinners (eating out, take-out, or delivery)		○	○	○
Contributions to churches or charities		○	○	○
Child care (day care, schooling, clubs, sports, etc.)		○	○	○
Alimony or child support		○	○	○
Groceries and toiletries		○	○	○
Cigars, cigarettes, and alcohol		○	○	○
Entertainment (movies, videos/DVDs, sporting events, night clubs, bars, etc.)		○	○	○
Pet expenses (grooming, veterinarian services, food, etc.)		○	○	○
Gifts (birthdays, office parties, holidays, special occasions)		○	○	○
Club, gym, or other membership fees		○	○	○
Haircuts and beauty treatments		○	○	○
Gambling		○	○	○
Other:		○	○	○
TOTAL EXPENSES	$			
What You Have Left (Subtract total expenses from net income)	$			

Your Marriage, Money, and the Law

Most couples are completely unaware of the legal ramifications of getting married. It's only after a tragedy such as death or divorce that people begin asking questions. Inquiring after the fact only yields information, not the ability to plan for such an occasion.

Being married gives you specific benefits and rights, including the following:

- Filing joint income tax returns
- Creating a "family partnership," which allows you to divide business income among family members at a reduced tax rate
- Setting up a trust specifically for married couples
- Receiving a share of your deceased spouse's estate
- Claiming an estate tax marital deduction

- Having joint home, auto, and health insurance policies
- Being able to sue a person for wrongful death or offenses that interfere with the success of your marriage
- Making medical decisions for your spouse in the event of severe disability
- Keeping you from disclosing private conversations between you and your partner in court

This list provides only a general suggestion of legal benefits. Please see an attorney for more information.

If either of you has been married before or has a child from a previous relationship, you may have existing legal obligations. Regardless of your past, make sure you and your partner have discussed and know the answers to the following questions.

1. What are the advantages of a prenuptial agreement, and what are the drawbacks of not having one?
2. Does either of you have a preexisting will or trust? Do you know the details of the contract?
3. Will you have one checking account or have two separate accounts and keep your incomes separate?
4. Will you add each other's names onto preexisting accounts and assets?
5. If you chose not to draft wills, do you accept the fact that the state will decide what happens to your estate in the event of divorce or death?
6. Are you marrying in a state that has community property laws? What are the advantages and disadvantages?
7. If you or your partner has been married before, who is *currently* the beneficiary of your assets, including retirement funds, government benefits, real estate, and personal property? Will you make any changes once

you've married, and do you know the proper procedures to make changes?

8. Are you aware that you are liable for any debt incurred by your partner?

9. If you've been previously married, do you still have any joint assets or credit cards with your former partner? Do you know the ramifications of this arrangement?

10. If your spouse passes away, do you know what rights you give up when you remarry?

11. Have you informed your partner of any legal or credit obligations you have that could affect the financial and emotional status of your marriage?

12. Are you aware of any illegitimate children or former partners who could claim a portion of your estate?

Financial Checklist

I t's often said that the love of money is the root of all evil. This may well be true. Money is also the number one cause of arguments between couples. The best way to reduce money squabbles is to create a sound financial foundation. Wealth is not necessary to achieve this stability. A couple with a very modest income can live comfortably and free from the burden of consumer debt, as long as they handle their money responsibly and agree to live within their means.

Together, complete the following financial checklist.

My partner and I have steady sources of income that enable the following:

○ Our own residence.
○ A joint checking account that is used to pay bills and regular living expenses.
○ A savings account separate from our checking account. (This can include any of the following: certificates of deposit [CDs], money market accounts, retirement accounts [401(k), IRA], or professionally managed brokerage accounts.)

○ Plans to reduce, eliminate, or prevent personal debt, including a goal of entering our marriage free from credit card debt.

My partner and I have discussed and agreed on the following:

○ A realistic strategy to be able to pay for our basic necessities in the event that either one of us becomes unemployed or disabled, or experiences a dramatic reduction in income.
○ An agreed-upon spending limit, debt load, and monthly payment plan regarding credit cards.
○ What our expected monthly expenses will be for the first year of our marriage.
○ Whose career takes priority and how much time and energy we will devote to each of our jobs.
○ How we plan to afford the type of lifestyle we plan on living.
○ Under what conditions we will borrow money, and where we will get the funds.
○ The terms of our prenuptial agreement or the repercussions we will face by not having such an agreement if our marriage should end.
○ Our wills, who our beneficiaries will be, and how our assets will be managed posthumously.

Finances
Thoughts on Your Answers

Money is a strange thing. On its own, it's indifferent. Money doesn't care whether it's being spent on food for the needy or bribes for the greedy. The irony lies in how extreme our sentiments and actions can be regarding this indifferent medium for obtaining goods and services.

For most married couples, money is about more than just dollars and cents. Each individual harbors deep feelings about making, saving, and spending his or her financial assets. Money can mean freedom for one person, but security or power to another. The goal of this section is to facilitate an open and honest discussion about what money means to you. In addition, you should have discovered the following:

- **How you will manage and who will manage your money once you're married.** Deciding how much you'll both contribute to your living expenses is step number one. Setting guidelines on all other expenditures and investments, such as how much to save and spend, is step number two. If you and your partner have the ability to agree on rules and goals for how you will use the money you earn, then you are well on your way to achieving a shared vision for your financial future.

- **The factors that influence saving and spending choices.** In the exercise "When Times Get Tough," when your finances suddenly became tight, what became your spending priorities? Did either of you refuse to eliminate in-house luxuries such as premium cable TV, because comfort at home is a top priority? Perhaps you were willing to sacrifice other areas to keep on track with your savings goals, because planning for your financial future takes precedence over any expense. Did you come up with compromises?

- **The emotional attachment you each have to money.** Perhaps you view money as a source of security and spend it cautiously. Maybe your partner feels empowered by spending. Understanding each person's emotional attachment to money will help you avoid actions that directly challenge your emotional-financial comfort zones. For example, a person who equates money with security will feel uncomfortable living paycheck to paycheck, while a person empowered by spending will feel controlled when being told what he or she may or may not buy.

- **Whether you or your partner is in denial about your finances.** Racking up credit card debt, frequent borrowing, relying on money from relatives, and floating checks are all signs of financial denial. They're the actions of people under the illusion that they can afford items and activities that are beyond their financial means. Not saving for the future, unpaid child support, and unpaid taxes are also forms of denial. These are signs of someone who refuses to acknowledge financial responsibilities and places the burden of payment on others.

- **How you both plan on earning a living and determining if realistically you can support the lifestyle you both desire.** We all have visions of getting married, buying a nice house, having attractive clothes, and going on vacation. But how are the two of you going to pay for all this? Laying out your first budget will give you insight into whether or not you can live within your means. Those admitting to "champagne tastes on a beer budget" know they have a decision to make: find a way to afford champagne or limit themselves to beer.

Part 9

Physical Intimacy

"Passion makes the world go round. Love just
makes it a safer place."

—Ice T

Someone once described physical intimacy as the glue that keeps couples together. The tingling, sensual desire you have for your future spouse is what elevates him or her from just being a close friend. When you take your wedding vows, you make an oath before friends and family to share these deeply meaningful ties with only your spouse.

Physical expression of your passion should not be seen as a pastime or a mandatory act of matrimony, but an expression of how much you and your partner mean to each other. Each one of you must let your thoughts and desires be known. You shouldn't rely on your partner to figure out what actions bring the most pleasure.

True and lasting intimacy is built over time, and it's achieved on many levels and in many forms. It can be purely sexual or also nurturing, comforting, and even invigorating. It is unique to each couple. Never underestimate the power of a subtle caress on the shoulder, or the pleasure of a light kiss on the cheek.

Although "it takes two to tango," each person's actual steps differ. Yet, they work together to create the dance.

What, Where, and How Often?

The intimacy you share with your partner is special and should only be reserved for each other. Physical intimacy is the sexual expression of your love and a gift you both should desire giving and receiving.

With your partner, ask each question and discuss your answers.

1. If this is your or your partner's first sexual experience, what are your expectations?
2. How often do you expect to engage in sexual activity?
3. How long do you believe your lovemaking sessions should last?
4. Where and when do you prefer to engage in lovemaking?
5. Would you like to receive feedback about your sexual style? If so, how would you like to receive it?
6. What are your sexual fantasies? Would you like them acted out?
7. Can you name a few things that turn you off sexually?
8. What places or situations get you in the mood for lovemaking?

9. What are the times or conditions when you do not wish to have sex with your partner?

10. Do you harbor any sexual fears or confusion about your sexual identity or desires?

11. What is your opinion about masturbation?

12. What are your opinions concerning the use of sexual games, "dirty talk," or toys to enhance your lovemaking?

13. How would you feel if your partner turned down your request for sex? What would you say or do?

14. How open are you to experimenting with new sexual positions and techniques?

15. Are there any actions you perceive as being sexually deviant or perverted?

16. What are your feelings about pornography?

17. Will you and your partner use pornography to enhance your lovemaking? Will you keep pornographic materials in your home?

18. Do you mind if your partner watches pornography, even if you choose not to?

19. Will you and your partner be tested for sexually transmitted diseases prior to getting married?

20. Do you doubt your ability to commit to a monogamous sexual relationship?

21. How will you resist the temptation to be unfaithful to your partner?

22. Will you use sex as a bargaining tool or to punish and manipulate your partner?

23. Do you like dressing in tight or revealing clothes?

24. How would you feel if your partner requested you to wear tight or revealing clothes?

25. Are you nervous about how you will perform sexually with your partner?

26. How do you feel about public displays of affection?

27. Are you open to making love in daring places? How would you react if your partner felt differently?

Let's Get Physical

Numerous studies indicate that married people live longer than those who remain single. Part of the reason is that spouses are live-in caretakers. They detect physical changes in their mates and encourage them to seek medical attention. Their nurturing also speeds healing and acts as an immunity booster.

Take turns with your partner answering and discussing each of the following questions.

1. Would you feel comfortable showing your partner a bump or rash in an embarrassing part of your body?
2. Are you comfortable discussing bodily functions with your partner?
3. Are you at an elevated risk for any diseases, whether hereditary or self-induced?
4. How often do you go to the doctor for checkups?
5. Are you somewhat of a hypochondriac?
6. How seriously ill or injured do you have to be to seek medical attention?
7. What is your favorite part of your body?
8. What is your favorite part of your partner's body?

9. Do you have any tattoos? If not, do you plan on acquiring any?
10. Are you frequently on a diet?
11. Do you frequently talk about being on a diet? routinely comment on the nutritional content of food?
12. Would you ever consider having cosmetic surgery?
13. Would you ever suggest that your partner enhance his or her looks through surgery or an extreme makeover?
14. Would you pay for your partner's cosmetic surgery?
15. How important is it that you be physically fit?
16. If your partner were showing signs of balding, would you say something to him or her?
17. Do you think it's rude to belch or pass gas in front of your partner?
18. Would you take illegal supplements to enhance your appearance?
19. What would you do if your partner snored and kept you awake at night?
20. Do you have any physical limitations due to an illness or injury?
21. Are you on antidepressants or other mood-altering drugs?
22. Have you ever been diagnosed with an STD?

44

What Would You Do?

Picturing ourselves in a variety of difficult situations can offer clues as to how we would react under given circumstances.

With your partner, try to imagine yourselves in the hypothetical situations provided below. Read through each description and discuss possible solutions you and your partner would offer each couple. Ask yourselves if the advice you offer would be the same you would follow.

Drew and Debra were high school sweethearts and married soon after graduation. Drew's job as a DJ requires him to attend several parties and work late hours each weekend to promote his business. He claims that flirting with women is part of doing his job, but insists that he remains faithful to his wife. Debra gets hurt and angry when she catches him giving other women the eye. Drew believes Debra is being jealous and possessive. Debra feels he is being disrespectful and needs to grow up.

Do you believe any of their accusations are correct? What would you advise this couple to do to solve their problem?

Juan and Janelle have been married for ten years. A bad back has kept
Juan from exercising as much as he would like. As a result, he has
gained quite a bit of weight. Although Janelle still loves him, she finds
him physically unattractive and makes excuses to avoid having sex
with him. She complains that he refuses to groom on the weekends,
because he believes it's his "time to relax." Juan complains that Janelle
is frigid. She complains that he does nothing to try to get her "in the
mood."

*What would you do if there were any dramatic changes in your or your
partner's physical appearance? What would you recommend this couple
do to resolve their problem?*

Brent and Brianna had been married for several years before Brent
confessed to her that he is a cross-dresser. Brent assures Brianna that
he's heterosexual but occasionally enjoys dressing up in women's
clothing and going out in public as a woman. Brent insists that their
sex life, which both agree has been good, does not need to suffer.
Brianna is confused.

*What would you do if you found out your partner had an unusual fetish
or sexual impulse? What would you suggest this couple do?*

Ali and Anna love each other and their careers. For Anna, a challenging
day at the office creates a desire for great sex when she gets home. Ali,
on the other hand, feels wiped out after a challenging day at work and
prefers to zone out in front of the television. Anna tells Ali that sex
once a week is not enough for her. Ali tells Anna that he's physically
too tired to perform as often as she desires.

*How would you handle differences in needs for physical intimacy? What
would you suggest this couple do to resolve their problem?*

Graham and Gina had enjoyed a satisfying sex life until their third child was born. Gina then declared that she had no interest in sex and would be perfectly content just hugging and kissing. Graham loves his wife but does not want to live a life of abstinence. Gina agreed to see a physician, but the prescribed treatment did nothing to enhance her libido.

What would you do if there were a drop in your or your partner's desire for sex? What would you suggest this couple do to resolve their problem?

Honor and Trust

L ife has a way of throwing us into little situations that test our honesty, such as when a good friend asks what you *really* think of his new girlfriend, or when the DMV asks for your real height and weight. At some point, you and your partner will find yourselves in a position in which you will have to decide whether honesty is the best policy.

Read each scenario out loud. With your partner, choose the option that best describes how each of you would handle the given situation.

1. Your partner's friend makes a pass at you. You
   a. warn him or her that you'll tell everyone about his or her behavior if it ever happens again.
   b. say nothing but enjoy the attention.
   c. tell your partner.
   d. say nothing and avoid the friend at all costs.
2. An old flame asks to meet you for lunch. You
   a. go ahead without telling your partner about the meeting.
   b. tell your ex, "No, thank you. I'm not interested in dwelling in the past."

    c. say, "Sure, but only if my fiancé can come too."

    d. ask for your partner's permission to go.

3. You would love some risqué photos of your partner, but he or she refuses to oblige. You
   a. wait until he or she is asleep and take a few pictures yourself.
   b. bring home brochures from photographers who do tasteful nude photography.
   c. tease your partner for being such a prude.
   d. get a computer image of your partner's face and superimpose it on another person's nude body.

4. A brief fling while you and your partner were on bad terms has left you with a sexually transmitted disease (STD). You
   a. tell your partner about your STD to protect his or her health.
   b. say and do nothing.
   c. go to the doctor and get treated, but keep it a secret from your partner.
   d. blame your partner for infecting you.

5. A friend secretly tells you that she heard your partner is having an affair. You
   a. ignore the news since your friend is probably lying.
   b. confront your partner and demand the truth.
   c. hire an investigator to follow your partner.
   d. believe your friend and cheat on your partner to even the score.

6. Your partner has been invited to a wild bachelor party. You
   a. hand him a roll of bills and say, "Have a great time!"
   b. tell him he can't go.
   c. tell him he can't go unless you go with him.
   d. get a trusted friend to go and watch his every move.

7. Your partner's job sends him or her away on business trips with members of the opposite sex. You
   a. insist your partner look for a different job or transfer to another department.
   b. travel with him or her at your own expense.
   c. support your partner's career without question.
   d. allow your partner to go, but make several phone calls to the hotel to check up on his or her whereabouts.
8. A coworker you find attractive has been flirting with you. It would be easy to have an affair and not get caught. You
   a. flirt back and have some fun.
   b. try to develop a purely platonic friendship with this person.
   c. tell the coworker to back off because you're happily married.
   d. report the coworker to your supervisor.
9. Long before you met your partner, you either had an abortion or gave up a child for adoption. You
   a. say nothing, and hope the subject never comes up.
   b. tell your partner everything before you're married.
   c. wait until after you're married to tell your partner.
   d. deny that it happened or refuse to talk about it.
10. You catch your partner visiting a pornographic website. You
    a. get very upset and make him swear to never visit the site again.
    b. show some displeasure but accept that "boys will be boys."
    c. cancel your Internet service.
    d. withhold sex from your partner in retaliation.

Physical Intimacy
Thoughts on Your Answers

Human sexuality is highly complex. Decades of research and countless books and articles (not to mention TV and radio talk shows) have tried to explain its many facets. People who believe that physical intimacy is purely driven by hormones are ignoring the important role that culture, past experiences, and self-esteem play in determining what makes us feel sexually compatible with our partners.

The questions in this section were developed to have you and your partner sit down and discuss the physical intimacy you desire and are prepared to give. Don't believe that without asking you can know what your partner wants and needs. In a famous scene from the movie *When Harry Met Sally*, Sally (in a very graphic and hilarious demonstration) shows Harry how incorrect he is in assuming he knows when he has satisfied his partner. By completing this chapter, you can reduce your chances of making such a mistake and can discover the following:

- **How comfortable you are in discussing your intimate physical desires with each other.** If you find you're too embarrassed to discuss physical pleasure with your future spouse, then you sacrifice obtaining information that could lead to a more fulfilling physical relationship.

- **How, when, and how frequently you expect to give and receive physical intimacy with each other, *and* if you're comfortable with this decision.** First you must discover what you each want in a physical relationship. Next, decide if you can live with these desires. Trying to change your partner's lax or puritanical views on sexuality is not the way to enter into a marriage. Decide if you can live with your partner's sexual style instead of thinking how it can be changed. If you push aside sexual preferences to please your partner, you'll soon feel the intimacy shared is one-sided.

- **Your psychological attachment to physical intimacy.** Did your answers reflect a view that sex is a natural act that shouldn't be taken too seriously, or a sacred meeting between a husband and wife? Take notice of the tone of your answers. Responses that were forthright, honest, and open for discussion suggest a healthy attitude toward physical intimacy. Answers that were vague or filled with anger, disgust, or disrespectful comments about previous experiences suggest an attitude that is unhealthy. Unless addressed, they could affect the level of intimacy you reach with your partner.

- **Who you believe needs to alter his or her behavior when your desires aren't being met.** Notice the preceding sentence said *when*, not *if*, your desires are not being met. In every marriage someone will, at some point, want a little more of this or a little less of that. When you and your partner answered a question differently, what solutions were offered? What agreement, if any, was reached? Beware of the person who will not take responsibility for his or her own satisfaction. They accuse others for not providing them with the intimacy they feel they deserve. They blame their partner for not being romantic enough, but do nothing to create romantic feelings within that person.

Physical intimacy is more than hormones, chemistry, or what goes on between the sheets. Peter Ustinov once said, "Sex is a conversation carried out by other means. If you get on well out of bed, half the problems of bed are solved."

Part 10

Emotional Intimacy

"Immature love says: 'I love you because I need you.'
Mature love says: 'I need you because I love you.'"

—Erich Fromm

T hroughout our lives, we search for a person to lift our spirits when we feel down, to encourage us when we need motivation, and to give us faith and hope when we're filled with doubt. A supportive spouse can do all this and more. Achieving real emotional intimacy means trusting each other with our most intimate hopes and fears, and feeling secure in our knowledge that we will not face these challenges alone.

Although the desire for sexual contact is great, the need for compassion is greater. It's not uncommon to see long-lived marriages that involve little sexual contact. It's rare, however, to see a marriage survive without a heartfelt connection between partners. The explosion in the number of Internet chat rooms and forums is a testament to the need we each have to connect with another person.

As a married couple, you must strive to create an environment that you both look forward to coming home to. Be emotionally available to each other. Listen to each other's worries and frustrations. It isn't always necessary to offer words of advice. Sometimes being an attentive ear is all that is needed.

The Real You

How you see yourself isn't necessarily how others see you. The exercise below hopes to prove this point. When making a selection, be honest about the less desirable traits you both possess. Everybody has his or her strong and weak points. Part of choosing a mate is deciding what shortcomings you're willing to accept.

Make four copies of the list below. On two copies, each of you will fill out how you see yourself. Use the other copies to assess each other. When you are finished, compare answers.

	Very	Somewhat	Neutral	Somewhat	Very	
Passionate	O	O	O	O	O	Stoic
Affectionate	O	O	O	O	O	Reserved
Trusting	O	O	O	O	O	Suspicious
Extroverted	O	O	O	O	O	Introverted
Spiritual	O	O	O	O	O	Agnostic
Confident	O	O	O	O	O	Insecure
Uncomplicated	O	O	O	O	O	Complex
Idealistic	O	O	O	O	O	Realistic
Serious	O	O	O	O	O	Silly
Calm	O	O	O	O	O	Excitable
Concerned	O	O	O	O	O	Indifferent
Judgmental	O	O	O	O	O	Nonjudgmental
Self-reliant	O	O	O	O	O	Dependent
Charitable	O	O	O	O	O	Noncharitable
Practical	O	O	O	O	O	Impractical
Impulsive	O	O	O	O	O	Calculating

	Very	Somewhat	Neutral	Somewhat	Very	
Cheerful	○	○	○	○	○	Depressed
Optimist	○	○	○	○	○	Pessimist
Responsible	○	○	○	○	○	Irresponsible
Law-abiding	○	○	○	○	○	Lawless
Conservative	○	○	○	○	○	Liberal
Reserved	○	○	○	○	○	Flamboyant
Loud	○	○	○	○	○	Quiet
Outgoing	○	○	○	○	○	Shy
Curious	○	○	○	○	○	Not curious
Adventurous	○	○	○	○	○	Staid
Fair	○	○	○	○	○	Unfair
Humorous	○	○	○	○	○	Humorless
Leader	○	○	○	○	○	Follower
Proactive	○	○	○	○	○	Procrastinator
Spendthrift	○	○	○	○	○	Tightwad
Reliable	○	○	○	○	○	Unreliable
Go-getter	○	○	○	○	○	Lazy
Takes responsibility	○	○	○	○	○	Blames others
Forgiving	○	○	○	○	○	Holds grudges
Aggressive	○	○	○	○	○	Passive
Controlled	○	○	○	○	○	Compulsive
Happy-go-lucky	○	○	○	○	○	Bitter
Social	○	○	○	○	○	Reclusive
Motivating	○	○	○	○	○	Discouraging
Lucky	○	○	○	○	○	Unlucky
Approachable	○	○	○	○	○	Intimidating
Friendly	○	○	○	○	○	Cold
Soothing	○	○	○	○	○	Irritating
Diplomatic	○	○	○	○	○	Dictatorial
Modest	○	○	○	○	○	Boastful

Showing How You Feel

Couples need to learn how to react to each other's moods so they can make good or bad moments better. Your partner is not a mind reader. Expecting anyone to automatically know when and why you're in a good or bad mood is setting yourself up for disappointment. When asked why you're angry, don't evade the question. Try to articulate the true cause of your moods. Unless you give reasons for your troubled feelings, your partner can't help you find solutions.

With your partner, take turns giving examples of a type of person or event that triggers each emotion listed; follow with a description of how you act out these emotions. Then discuss how you would like your partner to help you cope with your feelings and actions.

Describe the types of people or events that make you feel . . .	Describe how you act	Describe how you would like your partner to respond to your actions
hurt		
angry		
impatient		
confused		
lonely		
ripped off		
disrespected		

Describe the types of people or events that make you feel . . .	Describe how you act	Describe how you would like your partner to respond to your actions
exploited		
unappreciated		
inadequate		
silly		
resentful		
forgotten		
frustrated		
depressed		
worried		
intimidated		
suspicious		
guilty		
manipulated		
insecure		
picked on		
worn-out		
annoyed		
stupid		
vengeful		
embarrassed		
nagged		
loving		
undesireable		
sexy		
motivated		
lazy		

Saying "I Love You"

Few things are sweeter than hearing your partner express love for you. It may have been when he whispered "I'll make the coffee," or when she asked you to fasten your seat belt.

Taking turns, answer each of the following questions.

1. How often do you like to be told "I love you"?
2. How do you express your love for your partner?
3. How would you like your partner to express his or her love for you?
4. What makes you feel rejected by your partner?
5. What actions make you feel emotionally closer to your partner?
6. Are you comfortable expressing your feelings to your partner?
7. Do you believe showing emotions makes you appear weak?
8. How do you feel when you see your partner cry? How do you console him or her?
9. Can you give examples of appropriate birthday gifts for your partner?
10. When were you proudest of your partner?

11. Do you feel you have to protect your partner from the harsh reality of life?
12. How do you feel when your partner corrects you or says you've done something wrong?
13. When do you like to be alone?
14. Are you currently harboring resentment or envy against anyone?
15. Are you looking to avenge yourself against anyone?
16. If you could choose only two things in life to bring you happiness (aside from health or wealth), what would they be?
17. What type of emotional support would you like to get more of from your partner?
18. Do you feel confident of your partner's love when you're separated by distance?
19. When do you feel most vulnerable?
20. What lifts your self-confidence?

Are You Good for Each Other?

The joy we feel when we know we've found our soul mate can be heard in our sighs, seen in our eyes, and heard in our laughter. You've come together to support and inspire each other, knowing that you're better people and your lives have been enhanced because you've found each other.

Working alone, answer True or False to each of the following statements.

Your partner . . .

1. shows an interest in your day-to-day activities.
2. makes you feel like you're a good person.
3. makes you feel smart and resourceful.
4. discusses problems, ideas, and desires with you.
5. listens to your problems, ideas, and desires.
6. has demonstrated a desire to contribute to the relationship and make it grow.
7. shares your ideas about what you want out of life and how to achieve this goal.
8. builds your self-esteem.

9. tries to satisfy your needs.
10. respects your feelings and personal property.
11. encourages you to learn and pursue your interests.
12. supports and consoles you when you're faced with difficulties and failure.
13. is someone you can rely on.
14. makes your life easier and more pleasant.
15. is someone you respect and can look up to.
16. believes your marriage is a top priority.
17. has a positive and realistic outlook for the future.
18. maintains good relationships with most people.
19. calmly responds to crisis and adversity.
20. enjoys responsibility.
21. brings out the best qualities in you.

You . . .

1. show interest in your partner's day-to-day activities.
2. try to make your partner feel like he or she is a good person.
3. tell your partner that he or she is smart and resourceful.
4. discuss problems, ideas, and desires with your partner.
5. listen attentively to your partner's problems, ideas, and desires.
6. have demonstrated a desire to contribute to the relationship and make it grow.
7. share your ideas about what you want out life and how to achieve this goal.
8. frequently say things to build your partner's self-esteem.
9. try to satisfy your partner's needs.
10. respect your partner's feelings and possessions.
11. encourage your partner to keep learning and pursue his or her interests.

12. support and console your partner when he or she is faced with difficulties and failure.
13. are someone your partner can rely on.
14. make life easier and more pleasant for your partner.
15. are someone your partner can respect and look up to.
16. believe your marriage is a top priority.
17. have a positive and realistic outlook for the future.
18. maintain good relationships with most people.
19. calmly respond to crisis and adversity.
20. enjoy responsibility.
21. brings out the best qualities in your partner.

Are You Bad for Each Other?

Marriage will not turn a bad relationship into a good one. Drama and intensity in a relationship can be addictive, but it can also cloud our judgment. A love affair that's a roller-coaster ride of emotions may seem exciting at first. But what if you could never get off?

Working alone, answer True or False to each of the following statements.

Your partner . . .

1. depends on you for all his basic needs, such as food, shelter, money.
2. doesn't love you as much as you love him or her.
3. puts you down and belittles your thoughts and opinions.
4. is frequently involved in scams or get-rich-quick schemes.
5. evades telling you where he's been or who he's spent time with.
6. can't keep a job or has a history of employment difficulties.

7. has fits of uncontrollable anger or has used physical violence against you or others.
8. won't allow you to make your own decisions.
9. is suspicious about where you've been and whom you've spent time with.
10. is unreliable or untrustworthy.
11. is addicted to drugs, alcohol, pornography, or Internet chat rooms.
12. seems bothered every time you call or make a request.
13. depends on you to do all the planning or paying for any activities you do together.
14. has a "my way or the highway" attitude.
15. uses guilt to manipulate your feelings.
16. is misunderstood by everyone but you.
17. blames you or others for anything that goes wrong.
18. falls apart at the slightest hint of crisis.
19. frequently gives you the silent treatment or completely withdraws when you try to discuss problems.
20. engages in criminal behavior.
21. relies on you to bail him or her out of trouble.

You . . .

1. depend on your partner for all your basic needs, such as food, shelter, money.
2. love your partner more than he or she loves you.
3. put your partner down and often belittle his or her thoughts and opinions.
4. are frequently involved in get-rich-quick schemes.
5. evade telling your partner where you've been or who you've spent time with.
6. can't keep a job or have a history of employment difficulties.

7. have fits of uncontrollable anger or have used physical violence against your partner or others.
8. won't allow your partner to make his or her own decisions.
9. are suspicious about where your partner has been and whom he or she has spent time with.
10. have been called unreliable or untrustworthy.
11. are addicted to drugs, alcohol, pornography, or Internet chat rooms.
12. feel bothered every time your partner calls you or makes a request.
13. depend on your partner to do all the planning or paying for any activities you do together.
14. feel that it's "my way or the highway."
15. use guilt to manipulate your partner's feelings.
16. feel misunderstood by everyone around you except your partner.
17. blame your partner or others for anything that goes wrong.
18. overreact at the slightest hint of crisis.
19. withdraw or give your partner the silent treatment when he or she tries to discuss problems.
20. have a problem obeying the law.
21. frequently ask your partner to bail you out of trouble.

Emotional Intimacy
Thoughts on Your Answers

Communication is often thought of as the pathway to emotional intimacy. But this communication entails more than simply talking openly and honestly. We all know someone who excels at communicating his or her feelings, yet fails miserably at listening and comprehending the feelings of others. More important than just talking with each other is actively listening to and comprehending each other. Talking things over may make you feel closer, but it may also make your partner uncomfortable, causing him or her to withdraw. Unless you understand this, efforts to talk your way into emotional intimacy won't be met with much success.

The amount and style of emotional support that is given and requested varies from couple to couple. Yet, each of us is born with baseline emotional needs that must be met to keep us mentally healthy and happy. Your answers to the preceding questions have helped you explore the following three baseline criteria, which must be met to ensure a loving emotional bond.

1. **Affection.** Everyone has the innate desire to feel affection. Knowing how to give affection is as important as expressing how you would like it received. Some people are huggers, ready to show their love with a body-enveloping squeeze. Others show their affection in less physical ways such as cooking their partner a favorite meal. Be clear on how you and your partner *want* to be shown affection, and how you *will* show it as well.

2. **Trust.** All people need to believe that their thoughts and feelings will not be disrespected or ignored. You are never more vulnerable than when you are in love. You've shared your most private hopes and fears with your partner. You have been able to

develop intimacy because your partner showed you that you could trust him or her when you feel most exposed. Ridicule and betrayal destroy this trust. Encouragement and reliability make it stronger.

3. **Security.** Everyone needs to feel that someone out there is concerned about his or her safety and well-being. For example, a child runs to his mother for comfort after a fall. Likewise, you seek your partner for comfort after a bad day, or to share your joy in receiving good news. A loving, emotional connection deepens when you are secure in the knowledge that you and your partner will always be there for each other, and that your happiness is of primary concern.

Part **11**

Special Situations

"Am I united with my friend in heart
What matters if our place be wide apart?"

—Anwar I-Suheili

Not everyone chooses to marry the boy or girl next door. Some marry those behind bars; others, those in the public eye. Many individuals are attracted to their partners simply because they are in special situations. The fact that they can stand out in a group of average people makes them more alluring.

The men and women in our armed services are such a society unto themselves that they refer to anyone outside of their world of the enlisted as "civilians." Celebrities are under such strong pressures that few can endure the lifestyle without developing self-destructive behaviors or becoming divorced.

Marrying someone from another country gives you the opportunity to see your country through the eyes of a foreigner. When marrying someone in prison, you're choosing to live with the mores and attitudes of inmates and ex-cons.

If you marry someone much older or younger than yourself, you are accepting that you will probably have two diverse groups of friends who won't intermix.

51

Marrying Someone
in the Military

Marrying a member of the military entails both honor and adjustment. The armed forces provide their members with a lifestyle rich in tradition and camaraderie. Yet, this lifestyle also involves inconveniences such as frequent relocation and long periods of separation. Military life can feel confining for those unaccustomed to its discipline and overwhelming for those uncomfortable with change.

With your partner, discuss your answers to the following questions.

1. How will you cope when your partner is away on duty?
2. Will you go out with military people of the opposite gender, as friends, while your spouse is away?
3. How often will you write, e-mail, or call your partner while he or she is away?
4. How often do you expect your partner to write, e-mail, or call you while he or she is away?

5. Is there a limit as to how long you could stand being separated? If you were apart longer than this mentioned time frame, what would you do?

6. What would you do if your partner came back traumatized after a tour of duty?

7. What if your partner was seriously wounded in action?

8. What are your feelings about living on base?

9. Will you be doing most of the shopping and socializing on base? If "yes," will it give you a sense of community or of isolation?

10. What are your feelings about having to move every few years?

11. If your partner was assigned to a base you didn't want to move to, would you stay behind? What if you had children?

12. What would you do if your partner was away on duty and you didn't hear from him or her for weeks at a time?

13. If you're in the military, are you planning to reenlist? How would you feel if your partner decided to reenlist?

14. Will you or your partner be serving in the military as a career?

15. Do you want your children to grow up on base?

16. What motivated you or your partner to enlist?

17. What will you or your partner do when the enlistment time is over?

18. In what field of study are you or your partner specializing?

19. Do you have a career plan once you leave the service?

20. If you don't want to make the military your career, how will you use your military skills in civilian life?

Marrying a Noncitizen

Marrying someone from another country used to be an exotic exception to the norm. With national diversity spreading worldwide, it will be more common than ever to find couples where the husband and the wife are of different nationalities. For some immigrants, their nationality is only a country on their passport. But for others, it's an unfaltering source of patriotism that they retain whether or not they choose to live there.

For the sake of simplicity, the following questions were written as though your partner were a noncitizen. If you're the noncitizen, direct the questions to yourself.

1. Will you be marrying your partner in his or her home country, yours, or both?
2. Where will you be living after you're married?
3. What type of visa is your partner using to stay in the country?
4. When will this visa expire, and what documentation will replace it so he or she can stay in the country?

5. Is your partner staying in the country illegally or with forged documents?
6. What would you do if your partner were suddenly deported?
7. Will your partner be seeking residency or citizenship status?
8. How familiar are you with immigration laws?
9. How soon and how often will your partner visit his or her home country?
10. Will you accompany him or her on these visits?
11. Have you ever been to your partner's home country?
12. Have you spoken to friends or family who knew your partner before he or she left his or her country?
13. Will you send your children to your partner's home country for visits, vacations, or schooling?
14. Will your partner be giving up his or her foreign citizenship?
15. Who will pay for any legal or medical costs incurred by your partner's immigration?
16. How would you feel if relations between your and your partner's country became strained or even hostile?
17. Will you be sponsoring any relatives to become citizens?
18. In which country do your partner's loyalties lie? your loyalties? If they differ, will this cause friction?
19. Will you be socializing with other expatriates in your area?
20. Do both of you agree to follow all immigration policies mandated by the government? If not, why, and are you aware of the consequences?

53

Marrying a Criminal

For many people, incarceration has a personal meaning in their lives. They may be in prison, have a prison record, or be on parole. There are also men and women who write, visit, love, and make plans to marry a person with a criminal record. Although all individuals deserve a chance to show they've reformed, they can never divorce themselves from their criminal past. The chances for a happy marriage under these conditions are stastically very low. Realize that marrying someone that is or has been involved in unlawful behavior is a risky endeavor that can have serious repercussions.

Answer the questions below. When finished, ask yourself if you want to enter a marriage under the conditions described by your answers.

1. What would you do if your partner were sent to prison?
2. Would you stay married if your partner were given a lengthy sentence?
3. How often would you write, call, or visit your incarcerated partner?

4. Do you know your partner's entire criminal history, including acts that were not discovered by law enforcement?

5. Will your partner continue to engage in criminal behavior? If not, how can you be certain?

6. Is the plan to stay out of prison realistic? What actions have you taken to see that it becomes a reality?

7. Would you take your children to visit your partner in prison?

8. What would you do if you caught your partner violating his or her parole?

9. Do you believe your partner's crimes were "no big deal" or that he or she was framed or a victim of circumstances?

10. Do you and your partner see prison as a rite of passage?

11. Are you more attracted to your partner because he or she is in prison for life?

12. How many pen pals does your partner have? Is your partner receiving money, gifts, or visits from any of them?

13. Is your partner taking classes or learning job skills while in prison?

14. Once released, will your partner resume friendships with the same people he or she knew before going into prison?

15. Do your parents or children know your partner is in prison or has a criminal record?

16. Has your partner ever had a regular job?

17. What changes are you expecting from your partner once he or she is released? What will you do if these changes are not for the better?

18. Does your partner suspect that he or she will eventually end up back in prison?

19. What steps are you taking to ensure that your children don't get involved with crime?

20. What are your feelings toward the victims of your partner's crimes?
21. Are you marrying for the insurance benefits or to obtain conjugal visits?
22. Would you withhold information or lie to police or the courts in order to protect your partner?
23. Would you become a fugitive to avoid arrest?
24. What if your partner became a fugitive and you were unaware of his or her whereabouts?
25. Do you want to marry your partner while he or she is in prison or after release?

Marrying a Celebrity

Celebrities aren't only people you see on TV or in the movies. They can be presidents of companies, chefs, or top salespeople. They can be charismatic and outgoing or introverted and solitary, and their celebrity status may come by chance or after years of hard work. Fame doesn't add to your life; it exchanges some elements for others.

Working with your partner, answer and discuss the following questions.

1. If you're marrying a celebrity, how much privacy are you expecting to have once you've married?
2. If you expect to become a celebrity, how do you think the lack of privacy will affect your marriage?
3. Can you live with very little privacy?
4. How will you feel if friends or acquaintances give intimate details to the media about your relationship with your partner?
5. What if your partner wanted to keep your marriage a secret for "professional" reasons?

6. What would you do if you heard or read about an alleged romantic relationship your partner was having with someone else?

7. How will you react when you see members of the opposite sex making advances toward your partner?

8. How would you react if the public turned against your partner?

9. Have you spent time with your partner when his or her career wasn't doing particularly well?

10. What would you do if your career was prospering, but your partner's career was spiraling downward? What if this pattern continued for several years?

11. How many assistants or professionals will you employ?

12. Do you believe being a celebrity is glamorous and exciting or a nuisance?

13. Do you want pictures of your children to be published?

14. Do you want your children to grow up in the spotlight?

15. Will you primarily socialize with other celebrities?

16. How often will you attend public relations or other work-related functions?

17. Do you believe you and your partner have an image you must maintain?

18. How important is it for you to remain popular and held in high regard by peers or fans?

19. Does your partner ask that you tolerate behaviors that make you uncomfortable?

20. Are you expecting your partner to settle down and make fewer public appearances once you've married?

21. Are you marrying your partner to give your career a boost? because you think it will give you a lavish lifestyle?

22. Are you marrying your partner because you want to be a celebrity by association?

23. Is there something in your past that could hurt your partner's celebrity status?
24. Will you require additional personal security if you marry your partner?
25. Will you be able to do regular activities, such as going to the supermarket, once you marry your partner?
26. Do you fear for your children's safety by being associated with a celebrity?
27. Is maintaining your celebrity status more important than maintaining your marriage?

Marrying Someone Significantly Older or Younger

An age difference of up to ten years can be undetectable in some couples. However, an unusual arrangement exists when there's a generational difference in age. Marrying someone significantly older or younger than you can be a wonderful experience as long as you both mature together and avoid falling into a parent-teacher relationship. Answer the following questions with your partner.

1. Is your mutual attraction based on the strength of a single area of compatibility, such as sex?
2. Do you each have your own group of friends who closely match your own age?
3. Do you each have a separate group of friends who don't socialize together?
4. How does it affect your relationship if your partner has children who are close to you in age?
5. How do you feel having children who are close in age to your partner?

6. Are you afraid that in a few years you won't be able to keep up with your partner?

7. Are you afraid that you won't be able to keep up with any children you may have with your partner?

8. Are you afraid that your partner won't be able to keep up with you or any children you may have together?

9. Have you ever felt a generational gap in your conversations?

10. Is either one of you close to retirement?

11. Have you ever discussed how your life will change once you retire?

12. In the next ten years, do you expect to become more socially active or less so? Give examples.

13. Do you feel you're a parental figure for your partner? If so, do you enjoy being looked up to in this way?

14. Are you attracted to your partner because he or she is helping you to mature? What will happen once you've matured and feel you no longer need guidance?

15. Do you fear being abandoned for a younger mate?

16. Are you ready to mellow out or take charge of the world?

17. Do you become impatient with your partner's lack of experience?

18. Are you offended if your partner dismisses new trends or social developments as silly?

19. Do you believe your relationship is the result of a midlife crisis?

20. Do you feel you are being treated like a child or acting like a parent in your relationship?

Special Situations
Thoughts on Your Answers

This section has discussed some types of relationships that deviate from the norm. Everyone can agree that these special situations require more hard work than an average marriage. These relationships can work, but only if both individuals rise above the additional obstacles. You may not be able to control who you fall in love with, but you can control who you decide to marry. The success rate for special-situation marriages is not high. If you decide to enter into one, apply the following principles that other couples in special situations have found essential to their marriage:

- **A high degree of tolerance.** Packing up the family and moving every few years is not an easy thing to do. Neither is standing in long immigration lines waiting for documents to be verified. Couples that put up with such inconveniences do so as a token of their love for their spouse. It's their way of sending flowers with a note saying, "You're worth it!"

- **A high degree of patience.** Staying home while your partner goes on tour or returns to his or her home country can test any marriage. Couples that have endured long or frequent periods of separation suggest the following: Develop a strong network of friends and find ways to keep busy, such as volunteering or taking a class. It's easier to be patient when you have plenty to do. In addition to helping pass the time, you are contributing to your personal growth and your mental attractiveness.

- **A strong sense of loyalty.** Couples in special circumstances usually have strong forces trying to pull them apart. This dividing force makes them cling to each other and develop an ironclad sense of loyalty. To quote the wife of a well-known, desirable man, "If he spent the night at the Playboy Mansion, I wouldn't worry."

- **A strong will to stay married.** Individuals who enter unusual marriages tend to have strong personalities. They possess the courage to override criticism and the doubts of naysayers. The strength they have for their convictions also spills over to their view of matrimony. They can be pictured raising their glasses and proclaiming together, "Damn the world—we're staying married!"

Part 12

Your Wedding

"I don't want to get married, I just want
to have a wedding!"

—Shopper at a bridal salon

Planning a wedding takes a tremendous amount of hard work. It's a wonder more couples don't elope. Yet the thought of throwing an elaborate wedding is so alluring, that many brides devote over a year of their time planning the perfect event. In the past, elaborate weddings were reserved for first-time brides of wealthy families. Today, anyone with the desire and good credit can have a wedding that will rival Prince Charles and Lady Diana's.

The euphoria of the event can be addictive. It's easy to get lost in the romantic world of silk and lace, where you are the princess orchestrating a magical ball. But, creating a night to remember doesn't mean creating a night that will leave you broke and fighting with your friends and family. If you find yourself hawking family heirlooms to pay for decorations, or obsessing whether the napkins perfectly match the bridesmaids' dresses, then you've taken a plunge off the deep end.

56

Getting Married

Getting married can be exciting as well as frightening. Making a lifetime commitment is a serious decision that should not be taken lightly. It's natural for most brides and grooms to be a little nervous when they become engaged. But these brief moments of pre-wedding jitters should soon pass when they remind themselves of the confidence they have in their relationship. Unfortunately, not all brides or grooms share in this conviction. In the backs of their minds, they have a nagging feeling that marriage may not be what's best for them.

Answer the following questions alone before going over them with your partner.

1. What are your feelings about getting married?
2. Are you open to the idea of postponing your wedding?
3. Are you in a hurry to get married before you reach a certain age?
4. Are you excited about getting married, or do you try not to think about it?
5. Are you certain that your partner is the person you want to share the rest of your life with?

6. Do you feel something is wrong in your relationship, but can't pinpoint the reason?

7. Are you trying to convince yourself that your partner is the right person for you to marry?

8. Has your relationship with your partner changed since you became engaged?

9. Are you hesitant to make any wedding plans? Do you feel uncomfortable looking at wedding dresses or invitations?

10. Do you secretly wish someone better than your partner would fall in love with you and ask you to marry him or her instead?

11. Is everyone else more excited about your wedding than you are?

12. Are you only marrying your partner to please your parents?

13. Are you only marrying your partner because people tell you that he or she is a great catch?

14. Do you fear being let down by marriage after the romance of courtship and the splendor of your wedding has passed?

15. Do you feel pressured into marriage by your partner?

16. Did you give your partner an ultimatum, such as "Marry me or I'm leaving you"?

17. Are you getting married because you want to, or because you think you should?

18. Do you fear losing your freedom or identity once you marry?

19. Are you somewhat freaked out by the word *commitment*?

20. How do you feel about being called your partner's wife (or husband)?

21. Describe the perfect spouse. To what extent do you expect your partner to live up to this image? Yourself?

22. What makes you believe you could be a good spouse?

Your Wedding

Your wedding ceremony is the most elaborate and intimate display of your love. You are declaring your commitment to each other in front of family and friends. Whether it's fancy or simple, there's something magical about your first day as husband and wife.

With your partner, answer the following questions.

1. In which city will your wedding be held?
2. Where would you like to have your wedding ceremony performed: in a church, hotel, private club, or someone's home?
3. Do you want your wedding to be a formal, informal, or casual event?
4. Given a choice between a big but modest wedding or a small but lavish wedding, which would you choose?
5. Do you want your wedding ceremony to be religious or nonreligious? to have a theme, such as Victorian, medieval, or ethnic?
6. Which religious denomination will you choose for your ceremony? Do you actively practice that faith?
7. Will you be combining two different religious ceremonies into one?

8. If you're having a religious ceremony, does your partner want to participate in the religious rituals and prayers?
9. What would you do if your partner wanted to elope?
10. Do you want to write your own vows or poems and read them to each other during your ceremony?
11. How involved do you want your partner to be with the wedding plans?
12. How involved does he want to be in planning your wedding?
13. What would you feel if your partner showed no interest or desire to help plan your wedding?
14. Do you want to take a marriage preparation course or seek premarital counseling?
15. Do you want your pets to walk down the aisle or be members of the wedding party?
16. Are you expecting to pay for your wedding with money you hope to receive as gifts? What if you don't receive as much money as your were expecting?
17. How important is it to have a bilingual ceremony or incorporate part of your cultural heritage into the ceremony?
18. Is there any part of the traditional wedding ceremony that you don't want included?
19. Do you refuse to say the phrase "to honor and obey" found in traditional wedding vows?
20. Are you determined to have the wedding of your dreams regardless of the cost or aggravation?
21. How much money would you like to spend on your wedding? Give a dollar amount.
22. Will you be creating a budget and sticking to it?
23. How much debt, if any, are you willing to take on to pay for your wedding?
24. Will either of you be smashing cake in your partner's face after the ceremonial cutting of the wedding cake?

58

Family, Guests, and Attendants

Your family and friends are supporters of your love for each other, and should be honored to share your joy on your wedding day. Yet, well-wishing friends and good intensions from relatives can overwhelm you and force you to make some unpopular decisions.

With your partner, answer the following questions.

1. How much of the wedding are you expecting your parents to pay for? What if they offered you little or no money?
2. How much of the wedding are you expecting your in-laws to pay for? What if they offered little or no money?
3. How would you feel if your parents offered money, but your in-laws did not?
4. Who will pay for any additional expenses incurred the day of your wedding, such as additional food and drink costs and last-minute necessities?
5. If your parents are paying for most of your wedding, how much power will they have in making decisions?

6. How many guests are you planning to invite? How many of the guests will be selected by you, your partner, your parents, and your in-laws?

7. Who has the ultimate power to decide who is or isn't invited to your wedding?

8. Have you ever been a bridesmaid or groomsman? If so, what did you like or dislike about the experience?

9. Are you inviting business associates so you can write off your wedding as a business expense?

10. How many people will be in your wedding party?

11. Will any of your children or stepchildren be members of the wedding party?

12. Who will walk the bride down the aisle and give her away?

13. If you or your partner has two sets of parents (due to remarriage), who will walk down the aisle as part of the wedding procession?

14. Are you purposely excluding family members from your wedding, or asking your partner to exclude members of his or her family?

15. Will you be paying all the costs for your attendants to be in your wedding?

16. Will children be allowed to attend your wedding?

17. Do you want any members of your partner's family, including children, to be in the wedding party?

18. If your parents paid you to elope, would you take their offer?

19. Who will be responsible for writing thank-you notes? How long after your wedding will they be written?

20. Will you have any out-of-town relatives staying with you before and after your wedding?

21. Are you inviting some people only because you think they will give you an expensive wedding gift?

59

Remarriage

According to the U.S. Bureau of Statistics, in 1995, 46 out of every 100 weddings involved a remarriage. Of the 46, almost 50 percent were a remarriage for both the husband and the wife. There is no stereotype for second weddings because they encompass so many different demographics.

Take turns answering each of the questions below and discuss your answers.

1. If this is a remarriage for you, what are your hopes and fears with this relationship?
2. Are you always comparing your wedding or marriage to a previous one? Is either of you trying to outdo a previous wedding?
3. Will anyone who attended your previous wedding be excluded from attending this one?
4. Will your or your partner's ex-spouse be invited to your wedding?
5. Do you feel uncomfortable wearing (or having the bride wear) a traditional bridal gown?
6. Do you and your partner disagree over how formal the wedding will be?

7. How would you feel if your partner gave you his ex-wife's old engagement ring?

8. Will you be taking your partner's name once you're married?

9. Are you afraid of any wedding day sabotage by a former spouse or lover?

10. Will your former in-laws or other members of your ex's family be invited to your wedding?

11. Are you asking the same people who were bridesmaids or groomsmen at your previous wedding to repeat their roles at this one?

12. If either of you has had multiple marriages, are you still expecting wedding gifts from your guests?

13. Will you be having a bridal shower or bachelor party?

14. Are you sure your partner's divorce has been finalized?

15. Are you sure your divorce has been finalized?

16. Do your children approve of your remarriage?

17. Have you met your partner's ex-spouse?

18. Do you only know your partner's version of what happened in his or her previous marriage?

19. Do you or your partner keep any pictures of your previous wedding(s)?

To Have and to . . . Hold On!

Most of your guests will be completely unaware of what went on behind the scenes while planning your wedding. With so many people involved, all of them offering advice and making special requests, your patience will be tested.

With your partner, choose one of the answers to each of the questions below.

1. Your partner arrives at the ceremony still tipsy from his bachelor party the night before. You
   a. delay the wedding a few hours until he sobers up.
   b. give him an evil look and refuse to speak to him after you've taken your vows.
   c. pray he doesn't get sick at the altar.
   d. call off the wedding.
2. You notice a couple who never bothered to RSVP arrive at your reception. You
   a. greet them and say, "I thought you weren't coming."
   b. say nothing and forget about it.

     c. have someone tell them they may stay, but can't eat. Only enough food was prepared for those who RSVP'd.

     d. ask them to leave.

3. Your mother-in-law wants to wear something you find hideous or inappropriate (maybe even something white!) to the wedding. You prefer she wear something else. You

     a. accuse her of trying to outshine the bride.

     b. have your fiancé ask her to wear a different dress.

     c. say and do nothing.

     d. tell her she looks fat and frumpy in the dress and should choose a different one.

4. Your bridesmaids don't like the dress style you picked out for them. They've chosen a different one that you don't like at all. You

     a. let them choose their own dresses since they're paying for them.

     b. offer a compromise: You'll pay for their dresses if they wear the one you've chosen.

     c. tell them, "Sorry, but I'm the bride, and it's my wedding. You'll buy and wear what I've chosen."

     d. Try to find another dress you can all agree on.

5. You don't approve of the person your fiancé chose to be his best man. You

     a. say or do nothing.

     b. confess your feelings to your fiancé and hope he understands.

     c. demand that your fiancé choose someone else.

     d. get your fiancé's ex-girlfriend to be your maid of honor.

6. You're struggling with the guest list because only one more person can be invited. You decide to invite

     a. one of your friends.

     b. one of your partner's friends.

    c. a friend of your in-laws.

    d. a friend of your parents.

7. Your parents are paying for most of your wedding, but you don't agree with some of their requests. You

    a. tell them its your wedding, not theirs, and you will make all the decisions.

    b. agree to their requests because they have put up most of the money.

    c. give the money back so you don't have to do what they ask.

    d. compromise with them.

8. One of your bridesmaids excitedly tells you that she will be seven months pregnant at your wedding. You

    a. tell her she's not a bridesmaid anymore.

    b. have a seamstress alter or make a special dress for her.

    c. tell her that she can be in the wedding, but not in the pictures.

    d. say, "Congratulations," and don't let it bother you.

9. Your fiancé wants you to ask his sister to be a bridesmaid. You met his sister once, and didn't like her. Also, that would prevent you from asking your good friend from being a bridesmaid. You

    a. tell your partner to forget it.

    b. ask his sister to be a bridesmaid.

    c. include both his sister and your friend, even if this means having too many bridesmaids.

    d. tell your fiancé that his sister can dress in a suit and be one of his groomsmen.

10. One of your closest friends says she would love to be a bridesmaid, but can't afford the dress and accessories. You

    a. offer to pay for her dress, but keep it a secret out of fairness to the other bridesmaids.

    b. take back your invitation.

    c. look for a less-expensive dress for your bridesmaids.

    d. tell her to charge it or borrow money and pay it off little by little.

11. One of your close relatives habitually gets drunk and makes a scene at weddings. You

    a. ask her not to go to the wedding reception because you feel she can't control her drinking.

    b. secretly assign her a chaperone to keep her from drinking at the wedding.

    c. make her promise not to drink, and take your chances.

    d. invite her, but say and do nothing.

12. Your partner tells you that he would rather save money for a house than have an elaborate wedding or go on a honeymoon. You

    a. agree, and admire him for his thriftiness.

    b. say, "Forget it. We can buy a house anytime; our wedding is a once-in-a-lifetime event."

    c. say, "It's a house or me. You decide."

    d. save aggressively and tone down the size of the wedding and honeymoon.

13. A close friend never sent you a wedding gift. You

    a. ask him point-blank, "Did you send us a wedding gift?"

    b. forget about it.

    c. drop hints and hope that he responds.

    d. end your friendship.

14. You received a substantial amount of money at your wedding. You

    a. use it to help pay off the wedding.

    b. invest it.

    c. try to double it gambling.

    d. blow it all on your honeymoon.

15. Your uncle wants to sing at your wedding ceremony. You're not crazy about the idea. You
    a. say he can sing at the rehearsal dinner.
    b. say you're sorry, but you already have selected the music.
    c. tell him your partner doesn't want him to perform.
    d. let him sing; he's not *that* bad.
16. You received several wedding gifts you don't need or like. You
    a. return them for store credit or cash.
    b. donate them to a charity.
    c. rewrap them and give them as gifts to other people.
    d. keep them for the sentimental value. Besides, you may need them someday.
17. The best man wants to throw your partner a bachelor party. You
    a. absolutely forbid it.
    b. agree under the condition that there be no strippers.
    c. agree but send a trusted friend to watch over your partner.
    d. send someone with a hidden camera to later blackmail your partner and other guests.

Your Honeymoon

So much planning and preparation goes into a wedding that some couples barely have time to spend together during the process. Your honeymoon is a much-deserved time to tune out the rest of the world and focus just on each other.

With your partner, answer the following questions about your honeymoon.

1. Where would you like to go on your honeymoon?
    a. An exotic resort.
    b. An exciting city.
    c. A romantic local getaway.
    d. Nowhere; you would rather relax at home.
2. How long will your honeymoon last?
    a. A weekend.
    b. One to two weeks.
    c. One month or more.
    d. The rest of your lives.
3. Instead of going on a honeymoon, you would rather use the money to
    a. pay off some of your credit card debt.
    b. buy furniture or a new car.

    c. start a saving account for a down-payment on a house.

    d. None of the above; you prefer to take a honeymoon.

4. Will your friends or family be joining you?

    a. Yes, they're responsible for introducing us.

    b. No. Are you crazy?

    c. Yes, same location, but different hotels so we can have more privacy.

    d. Yes, but only for part of the honeymoon.

5. Will you be calling friends or family while away?

    a. Yes, I'll be calling my parents every night.

    b. Yes, my friends have requested a daily briefing of our activities.

    c. No, but I will call work to see how they're doing.

    d. No, the only time I will use the phone is for room service.

6. How would you feel if you and your partner got into a fight on the first day of your honeymoon?

    a. It would be just like a normal day in our relationship.

    b. I would think we were just stressed from the travel.

    c. I would wonder if this is a sign of trouble ahead.

    d. I would pack my bags and go home.

7. If you were honeymooning in a remote location, what would you do if you forgot your birth control?

    a. Have sex without any birth control.

    b. Have a friend send it overnight.

    c. Abstain from sex until we got home.

8. Do you want people you meet to know you're on your honeymoon?

    a. Yes, maybe they'll buy us drinks.

    b. No, I would rather keep our newlywed status private.

9. What would you do if you couldn't go away on a honeymoon?
   a. I would feel cheated out of an important event in my life.
   b. I wouldn't worry about it.
   c. I would insist we plan on taking a honeymoon sometime later.
   d. I would make a honeymoon at home by preparing special meals and planning romantic activities.
10. What would you do if your honeymoon wasn't as much fun as you expected?
   a. Insist on taking another one.
   b. Shrug it off.
   c. Think it was a bad sign of things to come.
   d. Convince myself that it was a great time.
11. Will you have sex on your wedding night?
   a. No. I'll be too exhausted.
   b. No. I want to spend all night with my guests.
   c. Maybe. It doesn't really matter to me.
   d. Absolutely, even if I have to take Viagra!

Your Wedding
Thoughts on Your Answers

Not a single wedding has ever occurred where someone was not offended. A groom may have been offended by a gift, a guest by the seating arrangements. With so many rules about who stands where, and who's supposed to do what, it's no surprise that toes occasionally get stepped on.

Your answers to the questions in the previous chapters brought forward your ideas on what kind of wedding celebration you would like to have. Your answers also may have suggested that you were in danger of making some common wedding faux pas. The following are some basic rules of wedding etiquette that should be followed when making your plans.

- **Never ask for money.** Do not include requests for money in your invitations or, even worse, request that your guests donate money to a honeymoon fund. Your guests are people you've asked to share in your joy. They are not banks.

- **Never invite people to your shower whom you don't plan to invite to your wedding.** In effect, what you're telling this person is "Your present is important to me, but your presence is not." If someone you don't intend on inviting offers to host a shower for you, then you must invite that person *and every shower guest* to your wedding. If you don't want to do this, decline the offer.

- **Don't treat your bridesmaids like "bride-slaves."** They are your companions during the ceremony, not hired help. Be considerate about how much you're asking them to spend to be in your wedding party. Don't demand that they spend a small fortune on apparel and accessories for your wedding.

- **Never invite only half a couple.** If you love Mr. Hudsucker but can't stand Mrs. Hudsucker, you still have to invite them both. They are a package deal, just like you and your spouse.

- **Don't forget to write thank-you notes.** If you think they don't matter, think again. I can guarantee that at least one of your guests will be checking his or her mailbox waiting for its arrival. The best way to ensure they get done is to write them as you open each gift.

The rules of etiquette are all based on one golden rule: Treat others in a way that makes them feel special.

Part 13

Marriage Builders
or Breakers

"There is nothing nobler or more admirable than
when two people who see eye to eye keep house
as man and wife, confounding their enemies
and delighting their friends."

—Homer, *The Odyssey*

You've answered and reviewed all the important questions. You
see eye to eye on every subject including family, finances, and
daily chores. You're in love and have so much in common that
you're convinced that you can easily overcome whatever hardships
life brings to your doorstep. Most couples enter marriage with this
same sense of boundless optimism. Unfortunately, many falter,
unable to live up to their promises of lifetime commitment.

Like most couples, you will face elements that will test your
devotion to each other. Some will be marriage builders that draw you
closer together. Others are marriage breakers that can weaken or
destroy your relationship.

Marriage builders are actions and attitudes you incorporate into
your day-to-day lives that foster a loving and caring relationship. This

can mean dropping old habits and beliefs while learning new ways to communicate. It can also mean gaining new insights on how to better communicate with each other based on your personalities.

Marriage breakers are behaviors and traits that make it close to impossible for a marriage to survive. They are characteristics detrimental to your relationship that an individual can or will not change and may be so serious that only professional help can properly address them.

Marriage builders and breakers are what separate the long-lasting marriages from the short-lived.

Living Together
Before Marriage

You may be contemplating living together before taking your vows. If so, you're not alone. Consider the following statistics provided by the U.S. Census Bureau in 2000:

- At the turn of the century, 9.7 million Americans were living with an unmarried different-sex partner.
- The number of unmarried couples living together increased 72 percent between 1990 and 2000.
- The number of unmarried couples living together increased tenfold between 1960 and 2000.

Cohabitation is a trend that is forecasted to continue growing at a fast pace. Most of the social stigma of years past has been lost. Cohabitation has even gained acceptance by many as a good way for couples to test their compatibility before getting married. At first glance, moving in together sounds like a win-win situation for a number of reasons. First, you get to see how well you get along when forced to share the same living space. Second, you can save money by sharing living expenses.

However, if you dig a little deeper, you'll see that living together isn't always as beneficial as it sounds. Even though cohabiters have practiced living with each other before getting married, they don't stay married longer or have lower divorce rates than couples who didn't live together before marriage. In addition, many couples living together never even make it down the aisle. Although most say they plan to marry their partner, 40 percent break up within five years, and 10 percent remain unmarried.

Although the statistics don't reinforce the perceived benefit of living together before marriage, the trend toward cohabitation is likely to continue. Couples who move in together with a wedding date set in the near future have the greatest chance of seeing their plans come through. For those with distant wedding dates or who plan to marry maybe-sometime-in-the-future, it's important that each of you answer and discuss the questions below before moving in together.

1. What are the reasons we want to move in together?
2. Will we set a wedding date before we move in together?
3. If no date is set, will we have a time limit to decide if we are going to get married? or continue living together?
4. If we break up, who will be the one to move out?
5. Will we have a shared checking account? Will we split bills equally or itemize them?
6. Will we make any sizeable joint purchases (car, house, furniture, etc.)?
7. Will we have a cohabitation agreement that explains how we will divide any purchases or debts if we break up?
8. How long are we planning to live together without being married?
9. Will we be less disciplined in using birth control once we move in together?
10. Will we try to conceive a child while living together?

11. Will our children from previous relationships be living with us?
12. What fears do we have about moving in together?
13. Will we be allowed to date other people while living together?
14. What will we refer to each other as: boyfriend and girlfriend, fiancées, or significant others?
15. Will we tell our parents that we're living together?
16. Whose name will be on the lease or mortgage of our home?
17. Whose things will have to go into storage or be thrown out when we move in together?
18. Is this the first time either of us has entered into a live-in relationship?
19. How important is it that we eventually marry?
20. What will we tell people if they ask us if or when we plan to get married?
21. What are the reasons we're choosing to move in together but not marry?

Communication

There has been an increased interest in the study of relationships, particularly in what makes marriages flourish or fail. Thanks to the formal scientific data compiled, plus a variety of television and radio talk shows focusing on relationships, couples today have excellent resources (such as this book) with which they can educate themselves on the myths and truths about what makes a successful marriage. All stress the importance of communication as a marriage builder. Yet, despite all of this information, we continue to see couples whose relationships fail even though they appear to communicate with each other. This leads to a startling question.

Can Communication Be a Marriage Breaker?

We can all recall a failed relationship where there was plenty of communication, and in some cases way too much, between partners. As an example, let's take a look at Dawn and Denzel. Dawn comes home from work and tells Denzel not to eat in the living room. Denzel tells Dawn that she's a nag. Moments later Dawn tells Denzel not to be such a jerk, because she had a bad day at the office. Denzel says he doesn't want to hear her whining because his job is more demanding and more important than hers.

As you can see, Denzel and Dawn are definitely communicating. The problem is that they are engaging in the type of communication that drives couples apart. Their verbal exchange exhibited all four of the characteristics of "bad" communication: escalation, criticism, deflection, and dismissal. These speech patterns act like root rot, destroying what's at the base of your relationship—the friendship you share with your partner. Let's take a closer look at each of these characteristics.

Escalation

This negative pattern can begin with a simple comment or action. The person hearing the remark snaps back and in a few short moments the couple is responding back and forth with increasing hostility. This verbal volleyball game transforms conversations into arguments, and then into full-blown fights. In the heat of the moment partners say hurtful words causing pain and resentment. Often, the original subject is lost or forgotten. A barrage of unrelated failings and frustrations are introduced into the discussion. The battle ends without any winners, and both partners angrier than before.

There is also nonverbal escalation. Rolling your eyes, having your partner "talk to the hand," ripping up pictures, or blaring music your partner hates are all ways to escalate an argument without uttering a word.

Escalation needs to be stopped before it begins. Both of you must practice self-control. Learn to bite your tongue and take a time-out when your emotions take control over words. Nothing is gained by delivering an insult. If one slips by, the recipient should stop and respond, "This is not going to turn into a battle of insults." If tempers are running so hot that one person feels he or she must leave the room or risk exploding in rage, let your partner know that you need to give it a rest until you've regained your composure. Use statements like "I'm going into the next room to cool down for five to ten minutes. When I get back, we'll continue calmly." Don't just walk away or say, "I'm out of here" and leave the room.

Criticism

Nobody likes being put down, least of all by someone he or she loves. The most damaging criticism is an attack on your partner's character. It almost always starts with "You . . ." and is made worse by generalizations such as "You never . . ." or "You're always . . ." Accusations using *never* or *always* are probably untrue, and they make the accuser seem irrational. Personal attacks directed at a person's shortcomings, insecurities, or misfortunes are especially damaging. Saying "Maybe you'd have a job if you hadn't flunked out of school," or "You would turn me on if you lost some weight," are low blows that do nothing other than verbally abuse your partner. Such statements don't offer solutions, nor do they encourage change; they have no place in any conversation.

If you must criticize, turn it into a complaint directed at an action, never at a person. For example, the temper tantrum is bad, not the person. Start a sentence with *I* or *we,* and avoid using *you* and *you're,* which can make statements sound like accusations. Say, "I get so angry when the room is sloppy" instead of "You're so sloppy, you make me angry." Complain about the behavior, not the person. "I feel neglected" is a complaint. "You neglect me" is criticism.

Deflection

Deflection is a form of defensiveness. Instead of listening to what a partner has to say, the respondent puts up a verbal shield to bounce back any statement made against him or her. If one person says, "You forgot to call the baby-sitter," the other bounces back an accusation such as, "Oh yeah, well when was the last time *you* arranged for a sitter?"

Playing martyr is also a form of deflection. Here the person plays the part of the long-suffering innocent, sarcastically accepting the complaint in exchange for a heavy dose of guilt. Such a statement would go something like this: "You're right, after cooking, cleaning, doing laundry, and working a ten-hour day, I can't believe I didn't have time to pick up *your* dry cleaning."

Deflection may be a natural defense reaction similar to fight or flight, but it must be controlled. If you can't think of a nondeflective response, say nothing. Deflection is just an invitation to start an argument.

Dismissal

Here, someone belittles or invalidates his or her partner's thoughts, feelings, or concerns. A dismissal may come in the form of criticism, such as, "You think everything is such a big deal," or a degrading statement, such as "Don't worry about things you can't understand." Whatever form it takes, dismissing a person's concerns will not make them go away, it will only bring about resentment for brushing them off. If your partner is a vegan, don't take her to a steak house for her birthday. If having a clean apartment isn't important to you, but is important to your partner, then you need to move it up on your priority scale.

Communication can and should be a marriage builder. The negative characteristics listed above can be avoided in your conversations. They're verbal bad habits that need to be broken. They may not disappear overnight, but if you recognize them in your conversations, then you can put a halt to their use. Learn and practice the skills mentioned in "How to Discuss Your Differences" and in the following chapter, "The Friendship Factor." Patience and determination will get you there. The result will be years of good communication, instead of unhealthy communication that can make your marriage miserable.

The Friendship Factor

As a newlywed couple, you may believe your focus should be on being a good wife or husband instead of being a good friend. You're probably thinking "Once we're married, shouldn't I be thinking about how to keep our love and passion alive?" Yes, you should continually stoke the fire of love. But passion is certainly not all it takes to make a good marriage.

Occasionally you'll hear a divorced person reflect on his or her failed marriage saying, "We loved each other, but we just couldn't get along." A marriage with love doesn't guarantee survival, but a marriage without friendship can't survive. If you analyze long-lasting, happy marriages, you will see a solid friendship at the root of each one. These couples share what I call the "Friendship Factor." They treat each other as if their partner was their dearest and best friend in the world, and in most cases that's exactly what they are.

Spouses in a happy marriage continuously tap into the elements that make up the Friendship Factor. They do so daily, often unaware they're doing it because it's become second nature. They would probably chuckle to see what they have been doing for years described as a behavior theory. However, they wouldn't deny that camaraderie was instrumental in their marriage's longevity. Following are some characteristics of the Friendship Factor:

- **Good friends are considerate.** Would you change the channel on the TV while your friend was watching his or her favorite program? Probably not, so why would that behavior be acceptable with your partner? Friends also treat each other with respect even when they disagree. Would you tell your best friend, "You're just a jerk who's too insecure to accept any of my suggestions"? Probably not, so why would it be acceptable to talk that way to your partner?
- **Friends turn to friends when in need.** Turn to your partner first when you have concerns or worries, and be supportive when he or she seeks your advice. Would you avoid your best friends at their time of need? Probably not, so don't do it to your partner.
- **Friends find ways to connect.** Good friends keep each other up-to-date on what's new in their lives. They also shop together and help each other with projects or hobbies. These points of contact keep friends connected and help build a shared history of interests and experiences.
- **Friends accept each other's flaws.** Look around at the friends you currently have. Why do you choose to be friends with them? Is it because they're perfect? Probably not. You cut them slack when they're unpleasant. In return, they're tolerant when you're less than charming. Since you and your friends aren't perfect, don't demand perfection from your partner.
- **Good friends cheer each other up.** They strive to be messengers of good will and cheer. Friends try to make each other laugh, and enjoy recalling uplifting moments. They aren't afraid to act silly or look foolish in front of each other either. If you can't be silly in front of your partner, then who can you lighten up with?
- **Good friends compliment each other.** The praise isn't always lavish. It can be a simple comment like "Nice hair-

cut." Sincere praise is always accepted, no matter how small the gesture. Each compliment is a deposit into your relationship's fund of goodwill.

Marriages that flourish and provide joy are the ones that follow the example set by good friendships. Although we don't celebrate long-lasting friendships the way we do marriages, perhaps we should. They exemplify how two people can maintain a relationship they value, respect, and work at maintaining thoughout years of change. Simply put, they are the types of relationships every marriage hopes to emulate.

Reasons to
Reconsider Marriage

I f love were the only prerequisite for a successful marriage, then there would be very little divorce. Divorced people woefully explain how their partners changed after they were married. Often they ignored warning signs in the rapture of romance, or brushed them aside for fear of making waves in their relationship.

Broken engagements are certainly difficult. However, of all the people I've known who have broken off an engagement or been dropped by their fiancées, not one of them regrets the breakup. All of them admitted that it was the most difficult period in their life, and they felt their tears and heartache would never subside. Yet, in time (admittedly not overnight) they realized that a relatively short period of anguish was better than a lifetime of regret. So, if you or your partner has any doubts, address them *now*.

Below are questions that can reveal thoughts or behaviors that practically guarantee a failed marriage. If either of you answers yes to any of them, consider it a red flag, warning you to reconsider marriage. Getting married is not an obligation; it's an *option*. It should be a source of joy, not heartache.

Working separately, ask yourselves if any of the following behaviors or thoughts have occurred in your relationship with your partner.

Has your partner ever . . .

1. made it difficult for you to go to work or interfered with your performance on the job?
2. taken money from you or refused to let you handle your own money?
3. made repeated calls or visits to check up on you when you're at work or out with friends or family?
4. punched walls, thrown objects, or otherwise broken possessions?
5. physically threatened or carried out threats to harm you, your children, your pets, or others?
6. struck you and apologized, promising to never let it happen again, only to repeat the violence at a later date?
7. followed you, regularly opened your mail, listened in on your phone calls out of jealousy or suspicion?
8. used force, threats, or humiliation to obtain sex?
9. isolated you from your friends or family or prevented you from socializing with members of the opposite sex?

If you answered yes to any of the above questions, you may be in an abusive relationship. Contact the nearest domestic abuse agency and speak to a counselor to obtain more information on how to protect yourself and family from an abusive partner. Seek the advice of a professional therapist before entering marriage.

Are you or your partner marrying because . . .

1. you're afraid this is the only opportunity you'll ever have to get married?
2. you hope this makes your partner settle down and be monogamous?

   3. you don't know what else to do with your life?
   4. your friends are getting married?
   5. you want to feel grown up and get respect?

If you answered yes to any of the above questions, you may be more interested in getting married than having a marriage. You could be too young or naïve to understand and manage the challenges of being married. A long engagement and an intensive course in marriage preparation is advised.

Have you or your partner . . .

1. avoided social functions where you couldn't drink or take drugs?
2. woken up unable to recall how much you drank?
3. undergone a personality change when under the influence of drugs or alcohol?
4. promised to give up drinking or drugs but found you were unable to do so?
5. become angry when someone accused you of having a drinking or drug problem?
6. missed work due to drug or alcohol use?
7. lied about your drinking or drug use?
8. found it hard to get through difficult periods without a drink or drugs?
9. borrowed money or sold possessions to buy more drinks or drugs?
10. used money reserved for paying bills or depleted your savings to buy alcohol or drugs?

If you answered yes to any of the above questions, you or your partner may have a problem with addiction. Marriage will not cure your dependence. You must seek professional treatment before you get married. Don't deny yourselves the right to have a clean and sober spouse.

Are you or your partner marrying . . .

1. to get away from your parents or an unhappy home life?
2. because you're dying to have a baby?
3. because you hate being single?
4. to have a change of environment?
5. to leave behind an undesirable lifestyle?

If you answered yes to any of the questions above, then you may be using marriage as a solution to your perceived problems. Marriage doesn't solve problems; it *intensifies* those that already exist. Counseling and a solid course in marriage preparation are advised.

Does your partner . . .

1. disappear when you need emotional support or assistance with even simple tasks?
2. avoid saying "I love you" or find it difficult showing affection?
3. avoid introducing you to friends and relatives?
4. make plans, take trips, or attend parties or social gatherings without inviting you?
5. still have feelings for an ex-partner or frequently talk about a past love?
6. place his or her own family's and friends' needs before your own?
7. avoid talking about your relationship or future together?

If you answered yes to any of the questions above, your partner may not be committed to you or your relationship. He may love you, but he's not showing any desire to include you in his life. Seek counseling together. If he refuses to go, decide whether you want to waste your time with someone who is not devoted to you.

Do you or your partner . . .

1. have sexual fantasies about members of the same sex?
2. find it difficult to become aroused by members of the opposite sex?
3. reject the idea that you could be homosexual even though you've engaged in homosexual activity?
4. choose to hide your homosexuality in order to marry and have children?
5. believe that marriage will make you forget your homosexual desires?
6. have a secret homosexual experience in your past?

If you answered yes to any of the questions above, you may be denying sexual tendencies and desires that will not go away with marriage. You must discuss these issues with your partner and decide if you are really willing and able to honor a lifetime conjugal commitment.

Do you or your partner . . .

1. believe that your ideas are better than other people's ideas?
2. blame others for any mistake or inconvenience?
3. hate being told what to do?
4. become very angry when criticized?
5. routinely tell people what to do and how to do it, even in casual social situations?
6. easily become frustrated with others, especially when they don't follow your directions?
7. find it hard to relax or not sweat the small stuff in life?

If you answered yes to any of the questions above, you may have a difficult time giving up control in your relationship. Marriage is a continuous routine of give and take; sometimes you will do things your way, and other times you let your partner run the show. If you feel unable to let your partner make decisions that involve you, or if your partner doesn't trust your judgment, then more time may be needed to bring democracy into your relationship.

Are you marrying your partner because you . . .

1. need a father/mother for your children?
2. need the financial stability?
3. don't want to be alone?
4. need someone to take care of you?

If you answered yes to any of the above, you are looking for someone to be dependent on, not partner with. Marriage is a team effort, not a parent-child relationship. You must possess the mature ability to take care of yourself and be able to resolve your own problems. Unless you can do this by yourself, you are probably marrying for all the wrong reasons.

You may not be aware of the tremendous amount of pressure that is placed on your relationship to ensure it succeeds. Family and friends press you for wedding details and gush about what a wonderful couple you two make. Well-wishers brush off your premarital doubts by saying you simply have "cold feet." To the desperately looking, you'd be crazy to let this opportunity pass you by. Any single diner at a restaurant will confirm what you've already suspected: it's a world made for couples. Making matters worse, there's a little voice in the back of your head saying if you drop out now, you'll never have another chance to join the world of Mr. and Mrs.

Knowing this, it is easy to see how some individuals choose to proceed with a bad relationship than to have no relationship. The time and emotional investment they put into their relationship make it very difficult to step back and take a clear, objective assessment of the state of their union and decide whether it's best to part ways.

Personality Types

Descriptions of personality types can be found in astrology, numerology, and, of course, psychology. Psychology categorizes personal traits based on a variety of factors, and uses them to explain behaviors and patterns of thought. I don't believe that all people fall into a defined set of personal characteristics based on their birth date or birth order; we are much more complex than that.

When analyzing your own personal traits, you may find that you're not a complete Type-A personality, but more of a B+. In addition to not fitting perfectly into a given character category, you may find that you resemble bits and pieces of personalities in several categories. We all can be a little controlling or introverted given the right situation. And, given the fact that how you see yourself doesn't always reflect how others see you, how can you define your personal characteristics with absolute certainty?

Here's a list of several characteristics that you or your partner may possess. They are personality traits, not disorders. Unless they're extreme and inhibit a person's ability to function as a civilized human being, you should not make it your mission to rid your partner of these qualities. The descriptions are intended to offer insight as to why you and your partner can react so differently to the same incident. Suggestions are also given on how you can live with the personality traits that give your marriage its uniqueness.

The Perfectionist

People with this personality type love order. Their mantra is "If it's worth doing, it's worth doing right." They work and play with intensity, and are strong in their convictions.

If You're Marrying a Perfectionist

The traits your perfectionist seeks, such as cleanliness, consistency, and discipline, are probably the ones you want more of in your own life. Take advantage of your partner's fondness for organization and let him or her take over projects that are detail intensive.

If You're the Perfectionist

Use your strong work ethic and desire for optimum performance in ways that benefit your family, not drive them crazy. Perfectly refinishing your hardwood floors is admirable. Not letting anyone walk on them is obsessive.

The Independent or Lone Wolf

Resilience and assertiveness are the traits of independents. They value their autonomy and have no problem walking to the beat of their own drum. They are good listeners and are very loyal, though they can appear aloof.

If You're Marrying the Independent

Be secure in the knowledge that your spouse loves you. Don't expect constant "touchy-feely" expressions of love. To the independent the fact that you're married should be proof enough of his or her love. Independents never do anything they don't believe in whole-heartedly.

If You're an Independent

Make the extra effort to compliment your partner for the good things he or she does for you. Wanting to be touched or sweet-talked every now and then doesn't mean that your partner is trying to suffocate you or take away your freedom.

The Dramatist or Drama King/Queen

This personality type revels in emotional settings. They love telling entertaining stories or being privy to gossip. They may claim to hate turmoil, but seek involvement in quarrels, whether by participation or by demanding to be told all the details.

If You're Marrying a Dramatist

If you're marrying a dramatist, understand that they enjoy chaos. They believe it makes life more interesting. They enjoy their sexuality and flaunt it. Gregarious, sometimes to a fault, they take pleasure in being the life of the party and are always looking to make new friends.

If You're a Dramatist

If you're a dramatist, understand that your partner may not share your love of melodrama. The volitility that feeds your rich imagination can seriously upset others. You may find it hard to believe, but there are people who look for a quiet and boring existence. Respect their right to do so.

The Worrywart

You can see the anxiety in their faces, when they furrow their brows or bite their lip. They wring their hands, pace, or look nervously from side to side. They can be talkative or suffer in silence, but they are always worried about a real or perceived crisis. If they buy a new car, they worry it will break down. If there's a flu epidemic in Mongolia, they worry they'll be infected.

If You're Marrying a Worrywart

Your plea for them to stop worrying only gives them another subject to get anxious about. Don't ridicule their concerns; they are very real to them. Their fear is a form of defense. By being stressed over possible problems, they are preparing for them. The last thing a worrywart wants is to be caught off-guard.

If You're a Worrywart

Accept that you will never be worry-free. Try to manage your worries without overloading your partner with distress. Categorize your fears by proximity. Unless it directly affects your immediate family in the next seventy-two hours, set it aside. Remember that you are an example to your children, as well. Be careful not to pass your anxieties onto them.

The Go-Getter or Workaholic

They are goal oriented and driven. They're determined to make things happen, and have no tolerance for those who drag them down. Work is their testing ground where they can prove themselves.

If You're Marrying a Go-Getter

Become part of his or her team. Be prepared to make sacrifices. Your partner's ambitions may require a lot of time away from you and your family. Work motivates them. The more projects they accomplish, the more motivated they become. Some go-getters confess a fear that if they slow down, they'll stop and never be able to recover their speed.

If You're a Go-Getter

Stay focused, but beware of prioritizing your work over your family. Your objective should be to improve your family's quality of life, not to be absent from it. Stay away from ambitions that are self-serving and boost your ego at the expense of others.

The Introvert or Quiet Type

You can spot introverts right away. They're the ones who work at their desks while the office is having a party. Introverts don't hate people; they just enjoy them in small doses. They're not closet extroverts who need to break out of their shell, and they're bothered by those who consistently pester them to express their feelings.

If You're Marrying an Introvert

Don't treat your partner like a psychology project. He may be quiet and reserved, but that doesn't mean he has a personality disorder. Introverts just don't see any value in small talk and truly believe that the world would have fewer problems if more people kept their mouths shut.

If You're an Introvert

I realize the difficulty of living in a world where chatter dominates, but your desire for silence should be handled delicately. Telling your partner to shut up and then withdrawing to another room will not produce a peaceful result. Let your partner know that you love her, but you also love silence. Also let her know, with a wink of your eye, that your signs of affection will mostly be nonverbal.

Lounger or Leisure Lover

This personality type always seeks the path of least resistance. Their competitive drive is permanently in Park, and their get-up-and-go usually refers to trips from the sofa to the fridge. They deplore schedules and to-do lists, preferring to get things done at their own pace. This relaxed attitude can be comforting or aggravating depending on the situation.

If You're Marrying a Lounger

Be prepared to take charge in most situations. Loungers tend to be followers. They may be all for having a party or going to the movies, but they won't be the ones making the arrangements. You may not become a power couple if you marry a lounger, but you probably won't have any power struggles either.

If You're a Lounger

Your optimism and charm are assets, but your lack of urgency can drive others crazy. Not everything can wait until tomorrow. If you find yourself putting off chores and relying on others to get things done, then you've crossed the line from lounger to freeloader.

The Giver or Bleeding Heart

If someone needs help, they're the first one there. When asking "How are you?" what they really mean is "What can I do for you?" Non-judgmental and armed with the patience of a saint, givers love taking care of others. They're neither competitive nor demanding. They feel that their problems are insignificant compared to the anguish of others.

If You're Marrying a Giver

Be ready to share your partner's generosity. There's always a cause that needs fighting for or a distressed person who needs help. Givers don't like being fussed over or showered with gifts. They consider themselves fortunate, and believe that the time and money spent on such frivolities could be better spent elsewhere.

If You're a Giver

Don't get so carried away with helping others that you ignore your own spouse and family. The daughter of a hard-core activist once said, "My mom was so busy saving the world, she didn't have time for me." Remind yourself that people who don't have problems also need attention. Let organizations or people know that your family comes first, and they'll have to manage without you (and they will).

The Adventurer or Thrill Seeker

If it puts them on the edge of danger or offers them a chance to test their physical or mental limits, the thrill seekers are ready to sign up. Courageous and bold, they live for a challenge and for the moment. Always on the move, thrill seekers love taking risks. Whether it's high-stakes gambling or deep-sea fishing, they impatiently wait for their next adventure.

If You're Marrying an Adventurer

Don't try to dissuade him with tales of disaster; it will only heighten the element of danger, and therefore the thrill. You can't get an adventurer to settle down, but you can expose him to activities in which your chances of becoming a widow are reduced.

If You're an Adventurer

Be responsible in your quest for adventure. If you're destroying property or threatening people's safety, then you're looking for a prison sentence, not a thrill. Don't dismiss the concern loved ones have for your safety by taking unnecessary risks or foolish gambles.

The Designer or Artist

Those with a creative personality are always on a quest for beauty and truth through their art. They take their ability to create very seriously and have a very personal attachment to their creations. They're sensitive and moody, but can demonstrate a tremendous amount of passion and emotional depth.

If You're Marrying a Creative Person

Happiness can be found if you act as an enabler to his or her creativity. Be warned, however. Their work can be so emotionally demanding that you may find your relationship seems to take a backseat to their art.

If You're the Creative Type

Make your partner your muse. Look to her for inspiration. She may not be as emotional and sensitive as you are. However, if she inspires feelings within you, then in her own way she's an artist as well.

Habits That Drive Couples Apart

Happy marriages come in all different styles. What brings one couple together can tear another apart. Some couples can run a small business together, becoming closer as they discuss market strategies and the state of their industry. Other couples can barely put up wallpaper together and prefer to work in completely different fields.

Habits that a particular happy couple practices may go completely against the advice generally given to couples to ensure a harmonious marriage. Here's a personal example: We've all been told that couples should never go to bed angry. This advice leads us to believe it is better to stay up and resolve your differences, even if it keeps you up till 5:00 A.M.

I can honestly say that my husband and I have found no advantage to following this rule. Arguing when you're tired and want to go to sleep can only make you say things you regret. What has worked for us is to stop our discussion, cool off, and try to get a decent night's sleep. I found it better to rethink and talk about our problem the next day when we're not tired and emotionally exhausted. After some trial and error, you and your partner will develop unique rules and techniques that are exclusively your own.

There are, however, some habits that are proven marriage destructors in almost every couple. They are responsible for the "irreconcilable differences" that cause marriages to fail. Following is an unscientific look at some of the most common reasons couples give for causing their divorce, and the habits that cause them.

Incompatibility or Drifting Apart

Incompatibility and drifting apart are two of the most frequently given reasons for the breakup of a couple's marriage. Increased negativity between partners gives a couple the perception that they have nothing in common, so they find ways to avoid each other and eventually find they've drifted apart. Pessimism, contempt, withdrawal, and avoidance all play a part in dividing a couple.

Let's take a closer look at these habits that drive a wedge between a husband and wife.

Pessimism

Also called "negative interpretations," pessimism is when one or both partners constantly look at the incompatible or negative aspects of their relationship. A wife accuses her husband of working late just to avoid seeing her. A husband accuses his wife of seeing a friend he doesn't approve of just to cause an argument. In the eye of the pessimist, the partner's glass is always half empty. Tired of being with a person who is a constant source of criticism and negativity, the partner finds ways to avoid contact and stays away.

Pessimism is a bad habit that can be broken. Before a negative statement is made, a positive statement must be made in its place. When debating on what movie to see, don't say, "You never like my movie suggestions." Instead, say, "We both love comedies, and sci-fi."

Contempt

Contempt is resentment and unresolved anger over feelings of being treated unfairly by your partner. It develops when a person feels constantly put down, unappreciated, and insulted. Resentment soon leads to contempt, a repulsion for the spouse, whom they feel holds oppressive power over their life. For example, a wife who has cut off all ties to friends and family due to her husband's jealousy will resent having given up her social network to appease her husband's insecurities. Like a country that revolts against its dictator, in due time partners full of contempt will rebel by seeking to create a life without their spouse.

Trust and proper communication are the keys to prevent resentments from beginning. Give your partner the freedom to pursue outside interests and friends without feeling that they are a threat to your relationship. Discuss problems openly and with a common goal of having them resolved. Avoid communication mistakes that result in negative feelings between partners, as outlined in "How to Discuss Your Differences."

Withdrawal or Avoidance

This habit is usually the culmination of failed attempts to find unity. Here, a partner simply withdraws or refuses to discuss any problems with the relationship. The television volume is turned up, the conversation is halted to do some other activity, or someone abruptly says, "I don't want to talk about this." Other times, attempts to initiate conversation are met with the silent treatment, or worse yet, the partner leaves the room. A more subtle form of avoidance is to quickly agree to the person's complaint in order to prevent a discussion.

People who avoid dialog with their partners fall into two categories: Those who fear having a discussion, and those who have given up on the subject. Fear of emotionally losing control, either by resorting to violence or by breaking down in tears, is why some avoid discussing their problems. Still others grew up with a fear of confrontations. For those who have given up, the thought of initiating conversation that will be a futile effort in finding a solution is reason enough to avoid a discussion altogether.

If your partner is uncomfortable talking over problems, drop any desire to have a heart-to-heart talk over the issue. Instead, focus on encouraging your partner to express why he or she fears discussions. Try to understand the partner's avoidance of hot topics, and create a method of communicating based on his or her fears. For example, if your partner fears ridicule, assure him that you still think he's the greatest, and you need his help to settle this dispute. Once, and only after you've found a way to work with each other, can you begin to work at solving your problem.

Infidelity

Couples must be aware that bait will be laid out for them throughout their marriage. Some spouses will have passes made at them, while others may find themselves in a situation where infidelity would be easy to achieve and hide. Know how you and your partner would honestly respond if placed into these situations. If you both feel you cannot resist the temptation to stray, discuss what priority monogamy has in your relationship, and what effect an affair would have on your marriage.

Infidelity, when perceived as a reason for marital dissolution, has usually been preceded by feelings of betrayal or neglect. Spouses who feel betrayed often seek revenge. Those who feel neglected use adultery to fill a void or to sooth their insecurities. Although you may believe that the greatest temptation to cheat comes in the form of an attractive coworker, or hot neighbor, the greatest risk for infidelity comes from engaging in activities that build emotional intimacy with someone other than your spouse.

Substance Abuse

Drug or alcohol abuse or addiction is the reason many couples seek to end their marriages. People with addictions are married to the substance they choose to abuse. Their spouse, family, job, and health all take second or lower places to their addiction. Many who turned a blind eye to such problems in their partner or thought their love could cure their partner's chemical dependency are crushingly disappointed. Sadly, the signs of abuse are frequently evident before vows are taken. Yet in an effort to keep the peace, or with the wishful hope that the partner will change once he or she is married or has children, the addiction is downplayed.

Although alcohol and drugs immediately come to mind when mentioning addictions, several other activities can become uncontrollable obsessions. Common but equally damaging compulsions include gambling, shopping, visiting Internet chat rooms, and viewing pornographic material. Realizing that you or your partner has an addiction is difficult to accept, but cannot be denied if the facts expose the truth.

If your partner's use of drugs or alcohol has affected your relationship in any way, or if you or your partner cannot be without drugs or alcohol for more than one week, seek professional counseling before taking your vows. Love or devotion to a spouse will not cure substance abuse. Guaranteed.

If any of these negative traits are apparent in your relationship, you should seek professional advice to see if they can be corrected. Unfortunately, many of these habits are caused by problems that are deeply engrained into your or your partner's personality. Never marry a person with the belief that you can change him or her.

Epilogue
Final Thoughts

Marriage can be a wonderful and fulfilling part of your life. All the warnings you've heard about marriage being hard work that requires sacrifice and compromise are true, but the payoff is a lifetime of companionship with the person you love.

Some couples mistakenly believe that marriage will be a continuous state of bliss, where doubts, disputes, and boredom don't exist. This faulty image of marriage is a liability to their relationship, instilling an unrealistic expectation that results in confusion and disillusionment.

A more realistic view is to think of your marriage as your backyard garden. You can't change the dirt in your yard; you can only enhance its natural condition. Likewise, you cannot change its climate zone. So, trying to grow bananas if you live in the desert would be futile. The more work you put into maintaining the grounds, the healthier your lawn and plants will be. There will be times when your garden looks tired and lifeless. The trees won't have leaves, and the plants won't have flowers. Yet, you still give them water, because you know that they will bloom again. You do your part to keep the damaging bugs away. You try to avoid treading too much on the grass so you don't create an unsightly path. With your partner, you'll plant new flowers and trees and watch them bloom and grow as they enhance the beauty and bounty of your garden.

Spousal Ten Commandments

Thou shalt not

1. put down or criticize your spouse.
2. negatively compare your spouse to anyone or anything.
3. make an important decision without consulting your spouse.
4. use sex as a bargaining tool or as a form of punishment.
5. use physical or verbal threats against your spouse.
6. lie to your spouse.
7. prioritize work, hobbies, or friends before your relationship with your spouse.
8. engage in behavior that puts your spouse at risk with the law.
9. engage in behavior that puts your spouse at risk for physical harm.
10. be physically or emotionally unfaithful to your spouse.